The One Who Restores

Latoya Kashon Moore

Unless otherwise indicated, all Scripture quotations are taken from the King James Version of the Bible.

Scripture taken from the New King James Version®. Copyright ©1982 by Thomas Nelson, Inc. Used by permission.

The One Who Restores
Copyright © 2014 by Latoya Kashon Moore

ISBN (XXXXXXXXXXXXX)

Published by
KASHON BOOKS
Kashonbooks.com

All rights reserved under International Copyright Law. No part of this book may be reproduced or transmitted in any form or by any means without written permission from the author. Printed in the United States of America.

Dedication

This book is dedicated to the love my life; my husband, Ryan Scott Moore, who is my rock, my Boaz, my friend, and my motivation. Thank you for making me feel like your treasured jewel and helping me through my restoration process.

To my mother Freda Worthon, thank you for being my spiritual counselor. You have guided me throughout my life towards understanding my spirit and the ways in which God speaks.

To my sister Stephanie Worthon, thank you for believing in me and inspiring me to write. You have been a blessing throughout this entire process.

And to my dear friend, Michael Anthony Thomas Jr., your enduring memories that you gave me will never be lost. Your life has meant so much to me because you taught me so much about God and myself. Your cherished friendship will be greatly missed.

Contents

FOREWORD	5
INTRODUCTION	8
CHAPTER 1 THE ACCIDENT	11
CHAPTER 2 WHAT HAPPENS NEXT?	18
CHAPTER 3 THE PHONE CALL FROM HEAVEN	32
CHAPTER 4 DONOVAN, THE TEACHER	45
CHAPTER 5 WATCH OUT FOR HINDRANCES	68
CHAPTER 6 THE BREAK UP	77
CHAPTER 7 THE PROPHECY	95
CHAPTER 8 MEETING MR. RIGHT	102
CHAPTER 9 SWEEPING ME OFF MY FEET	120
CHAPTER 10 GOD CAN DO A QUICK WORK	129
CHAPTER 11 LEARNING TO TRUST GOD	141
CHAPTER 12 GOD SPEAKS	148

Foreword

Have you ever experienced a loss so great that every morning you were shocked with the recurring reality that the nightmare was real? Have you ever been so depressed that eating, sleeping, and showering vanished from your list of priorities? What about this one?: Have you ever encountered the seemingly impossible quest of connecting your emotions and spirit to the "It's gonna be okay" quotes and scriptures with which your head was so familiar?

Being a witness of Mrs. Moore's life through the occurrences found in *The One Who Restores*, we are confident that this book holds powerful keys to healing, restoration, and wholeness. Let's be honest: the most interesting stories are the ones packed with drama, tears, and a happy ending! All three of these elements are demonstrated in the following pages! Through the darkest season of Latoya Moore's life, she has gained wisdom that is sure to impact the multitudes.

As you read this book, you will embark upon a journey of love, despair, brokenness, and the ultimate healing and restoration. Get ready to discover how to navigate the route through your tunnel, whatever it may be, into the light of hope, faith, and wholeness.

-Kirstie and Kristie Bronner

I Corinthians 13 (NKJV)

LOVE

¹Through I speak with the tongues of men and of angels, but have not love, I have become sounding brass or a clanging cymbal.
²And though I have the gift of prophecy, and understand all mysteries and all knowledge, and though I have all faith, so that I could remove mountains, but have not love, I am nothing.
³And though I bestow all my goods to feed the poor, and though I give my body to be burned, but have not love, it profits me nothing.
⁴Love suffers long and is kind; love does not envy; love does not parade itself, is not puffed up;
⁵does not behave rudely, does not seek its own, is not provoked, thinks no evil;
⁶does not rejoice in iniquity, but rejoices in the truth;
⁷bears all things, believes all things, hopes all things, endures all things.

⁸Love never fails. But whether there are prophecies, they will fail; whether there are tongues, they will cease; whether there is knowledge, it will vanish away.
⁹For we know in part and we prophesy in part,
¹⁰But when that which is perfect has come, then that which is in part will be done way.
¹¹When I was a child, I spoke as a child, I understood as a child, I thought as a child; but when I became a man, I put away childish things.
¹²For now we see in a mirror, dimly, but then face to face. Now I know in part, but then I shall know just as I also am known.
¹³And now abide faith, hope, and love, these three; but the greatest of these is love.

INTRODUCTION

It all started with a prayer to God, "Yes Lord I will do your will. Teach me your way. Yes Lord, I give you my life; use me as your vessel. No matter the difficulty of the journey, no matter which friends have to leave, or what relationships I have to leave-my heart will still say yes to you Lord." I prayed a seemingly simple prayer, but over time I realized that this prayer has locked within it a deep meaning, because of the relationship I share with God. The fullness of power in that prayer has radically and completely changed my life. That's the thing-when you make commitments to God, you have to be fully and relentlessly committed when you say yes, because He will take you at your word and that can mean that you will have to go through complicated situations to get you where God needs you to be.

    On my spiritual journey I've faced struggles similar to those of Job while struggling with a lack of confidence like Moses. Job is the central character in the book of Job. Job is described as a righteous man blessed with wealth, children, and good health. Satan asks God to challenge Job's character by taking away his good health, wealth, and children. God gives Satan permission to take away his health, wealth, and his children, but not his life. Although Job goes through those difficult trials in his life, he doesn't curse God, but rather curses the day he was born. God blesses Job with more children, wealth, and good health for his faithfulness and obedience to God. Thus, restoring all that was lost.

Moses, on the other hand struggled with his confidence. God asked Moses to go back to Egypt to tell Pharaoh to free the Israelites. In short, Moses said, "Surely not me God. I can't speak well. Why not ask my brother who is more elegant in his speech." As you read my book you will discover how similar my life is to Job's life, because the things that I held dear to my heart were taken away, but God restored all things that were taken away. I can relate to Moses, because even while I'm writing this book my thoughts are, "God, I'm not good at grammar. Who will buy my book? No one knows who I am. How will they know that my testimony is something they need to read about? Who am I?"

As I sit here pondering about my past, present, and future I find that I am left with only questions- questions, questions, and more questions about the unknown because the unthinkable happened. My first love was tragically taken away from this life. I didn't understand why this young, 24 year old young man was in a car accident leaving behind his family, and future wife. What do you do when your world seems like its crashing down? How do you react when you ask his family questions, but their answers give you no closure? All that is seemingly left is memories, feelings of joy, feelings of pain, and picture frames filled with photographs of the man your heart misses that remind you of the smiles and giggles once shared that are now nothing more than memories.

No one knew Donovan the way that I did. Some knew him as Camera Man, brother, friend, son, nephew, grandson, cousin, and student. There are many names they knew him by, but I knew him as confident, love of my life, Christian man, and teacher. As you read my story, I hope that you will understand my pain so that you may grow as I grow in this lesson. This is my life naked and unashamed in hopes that it will help someone else. God has forgiven me for mistakes that I've made and He has restored me. God continues to speak to me daily and I pray that you will ask God to speak to you in a unique way. I believe that as I share a part of me with you, you will begin to apply my life principles to your own journey, and in doing so you will free me as you free yourself. So, liberate me as we remember our dear beloved Donovan.

CHAPTER ONE

THE ACCIDENT

Most fairytales begin with "Once Upon a Time" but my story does not- it begins with Memorial Day. I was heading to a church retreat when I received a frightening phone call from Mr. Black, Donovan's grandfather. As soon as I realized that I missed at least three phone calls from Mr. Black my heart started pounding because no one from Donovan's family has ever called me so many times consecutively. As I dialed Mr. Black's phone number, I was interrupted by another incoming call from him. With shaking hands, I reluctantly picked up the phone and said, "Hello?" Mr. Black replied, "Sweetie I don't know how to say this…but

Donovan was killed in a car accident this morning."

The resounding ring of silence was all that I could hear. I felt as though the world around me had fallen silent and with a trembling voice I replied, apprehensively, with the only words I could find "What? I don't understand?" Mr. Black asked, "Are you saying what because you didn't hear me, or because you can't believe what I'm saying?" In a state of complete and utter confusion I told Mr. Black that I couldn't believe what he was saying to me! My heart immediately felt burdened. My muscles tensed with fear and my head started spinning with anxiety and nervousness. My palms began to sweat and as I shut my phone my eyes welled with tears. My chest felt heavy and it became hard to breathe. In that moment, the only thing that mattered was getting back home. I cried non-stop on what felt like the longest car ride of my life as I swiftly returned to be with Donovan's family. I have experienced pain in my life, but this pain was a new type of pain. It was more than physical, it was emotional. It took everything that I had to move. It was unbearable and easily became the greatest pain I had ever felt in my life.

I can't remember much about the drive to Donovan's house except that it was raining outside and there was a deer in the middle of his street. Each breath I took felt surreal. My hands were shaking and my heart was pounding so loudly that I thought it was going to burst out of my chest. Finally arriving at his house, I paused in the car to brace myself for the river of emotions I knew would begin flowing when I saw his family. I stepped out of the car and tried to lock the door, but the keys slipped from my quivering hands and landed on the ground. The first person I saw waiting at the front door with her arms opened wide was Donovan's grandmother, Mrs. Black. As soon as she hugged me my tears began to flow quickly as she whispered in my ear, "Be strong for his mother."

    I walked inside and I felt an overwhelming sense of sadness filling the house and thickening the air. I hugged Donovan's mother and tears began to fall from my eyes like bullets and soon we were crying together. Words cannot express the agony I felt in my soul. He was here one minute and gone the next. I've always heard people talk about how short life is, but in that moment, those words took on a new meaning and I understood them in a way I was previously unable to understand them. All day I stayed with Donavon's family as we mourned the loss of the sweetest spirit that ever lived.

After being with his family all day I drove myself to my three-bedroom home. The house seemed unusually empty and it made me feel lonelier than I ever have in my life. As I sat alone feeling empty and confused, I remembered that Donovan's parents brought over a bottle of wine and a bottle opener when they came over for dinner a couple of months ago. I figured that I would open the bottle that night. Although I had never tasted wine, or any alcohol for that matter, I grabbed a glass and filled it several times. I hated the taste, but I continued to drink because it began to ease the pain that I felt. My mind was deceived into thinking what I needed could be found in the bottom of the bottle. I poured and I drank, then I poured and drank some more, when there was no more to pour I began to have a conversation with Donovan (ignorant to the reality that he wasn't there). I started crying out to him only to find that doing so couldn't relieve the pain that was consuming both my body and mind. When my friend came over to console me, he was shocked to find me broken and in a state of drunkenness. The brokenness was expected, but he was expecting sober brokenness. Needless to say I finished the bottle of wine but waking up the next day wasn't easy. I realized that in reality, drinking the wine did nothing to ease my pain and I had no desire to ever drink again, because it did nothing for me but numb the pain for a couple of hours. I can now better understand why people turn to drugs and alcohol because it takes you to another place, but in reality your pain still exists. I asked God to forgive me for the mistake I made by getting drunk.

Throughout the next couple of nights I was restless managing to only get two hours of sleep. While awake for most of the night, God began to speak to me. He gave me the words for a poem that I read for Donovan at his funeral titled "A Blessing."

A BLESSING

What do you do when you want to ask God, why?
Why did this happen to me?
Why did you take my love away from me?
Why did you allow this to happen to me?
What I have learned, is the only thing that you can do, is to stop asking God why and start counting your many blessing.
Through tragedy there is still joy.
Joy from all the loving memories that God allowed you to have with a person.
Memories of the way you met.
Memories of the awkward quirks about that person that you learned to love.
Memories of the corny jokes that made you laugh.
Memories of the romantic gestures.
Memories of your Godly conversations.
Memories of discovering each other's' fears.
Memories of exploring new adventures together.
Memories of meeting the family.
Memories of all the inside jokes you shared.
Each memory is a cherished blessing from God.
We must always remember that we are only stewards over the gifts from God.

We don't own our children, our spouse, our car, our homes, or any possessions.
So when God calls home a spouse or child we must thank God for the blessings He gave us through the time we shared with that person.

CHAPTER TWO

WHAT HAPPENS NEXT?

Although the relationship that Donovan and I had wasn't perfect, we were a blessing to each other's lives and no one knows the type of relationship we held together. We knew each other's secrets, fears, dreams, and desires. We made future plans to open up a business together. Donovan went back to school to gain more knowledge in finance so that he could run the financial aspect of the business. In fact, Donovan planned to propose to me on my birthday, which was one month before he was taken from me. Donovan was my best friend and the love of my life for three and a half years. I had never lost anyone who shared the type of intimate relationship that Donavan and I had. We had plans, but our plans were not God's plans for our lives. It makes me wonder, who are we to plan our futures and get mad at God when our plans are throttled? This is why we must always pray to God for guidance and to order our footsteps every day.

As I sit here in the loneliness of my home, I remember meeting Donovan at my church. I met him after attending the seven day prayer consecration with my church. I traveled to the church for 5:00 a.m. prayer for a week. I later found out that he was also going to the prayer consecration at church. The very next week is when I met Donovan. He loved telling the story about how we first met. He would tell our friends that we met at the beautiful gate as we crossed paths by making eye contact. The beautiful gate name is based on Nehemiah chapter three of the bible. Donovan was casually mumbling to himself about not wanting to go to work and I jumped in his conversation and said, "Whoa, I don't work to go to work tomorrow either." That comment sparked one of many conversations to come. He talked as he walked me all the way to my car.

Donovan and I talked for three hours outside and he didn't even ask me for my phone number. He asked me for my last name so that he could find me on Facebook. I was definitely surprised, because it was unusual for a man to ask me for my last name instead of my phone number. Later, he informed me that he was afraid to ask for my phone number because he thought I would say no. I told him that I wouldn't have talked to him for three hours if I wasn't interested in him. We started to hang out at each other's houses and watch movies. We began to grow closer as friends as we began to explore each other's secrets and fears. Donovan told me he was a virgin and I found it rare for a man his age to be a virgin. I applauded his diligence and commitment to remain faithful to God.

After Donovan's passing, I prayed "Lord what is my purpose in life? Lord I give myself away; use me as your vessel. Lord, I need your strength to make it through." I realized that only through God's strength and unconditional love could I continue living. Not a day went by where sadness couldn't paralyze me and make me stay in bed, a prisoner to my own thought that "nobody loved me." Every day I kissed Donovan's picture that was posted in my room and thought about what I wouldn't give for another one of his juicy kisses. I knew I would never be able to smell him, hear his voice, feel his beard, or cuddle with him again. It's the little things in life that make each person special. The heart dies a slow death when you truly love someone and they're suddenly taken away from you.

My hunger escaped me and I had no appetite for weeks. I couldn't sleep well for the next few months because when I tried to sleep flashbacks of Donovan crept their way into the confines of my memory forcing me to stay awake. I had flashbacks of how we first met, the first time he asked me out, our spiritual growth, the times we spent with our families, riding the greyhound, birthday celebrations, dancing, and our snowball fight. Time and memories are some of the greatest gifts that God has given us. I've learned that we can't take time for granted because once your time is gone you can never get it back. One of my greatest fears is that I will begin to forget details about Donovan, or forget some of the cherished memories.

October, Donovan's birthday month came around quickly. We were still friends at the time, but I thought I would surprise him for his birthday. It was a sunny day and I surprised Donovan by taking him to a picnic at Piedmont Park. In the picnic basket I packed Kroger sub sandwiches, chips and cookies. We walked around the park and admired the nature around us. We laid down on the blanket and we watched the clouds move around in the sky. Afterwards, I took him to a movie and back to my house. I made my famous Pineapple Dream Cake that has a layer of vanilla custard with cool whipped topping, then I sang Happy 22nd Birthday to him and he blew out the candles.

  November was the next big month for us. This was the month that he finally officially asked me out. His family had already considered me his girlfriend, but it wasn't official. Donovan took me to Gladys Knight Chicken and Waffles in downtown Atlanta. I ate wings and fries, and he had the smothered chicken with mash potatoes and gravy. As we were walking back to the car, he grabbed my hand and asked, "Would you consider being my girlfriend?" I smiled at him and answered, "Finally…of course I will be your girlfriend!" Donovan had a huge smile on his face as he drove me home. He always counted the first time that we met each other as the first day that we started going out, but I always considered the day he asked me to be his girlfriend the first day we started going out. After the first day we met we never let a day go by without seeing each other, even if it was only for an hour. He was everything that I prayed for in a Christian boyfriend. He had the sweetest spirit that I had ever seen, he was kind hearted, patient, caring, family oriented, hardworking, he adored me, and most importantly he loved God with all of his heart.

During November Donovan helped me move into my first apartment with a roommate. He was adamant at helping me financially with my first apartment by offering me a couple hundred dollars each month. Donovan's family helped with some of the furniture in my apartment. Donovan and I continued to grow closer to each other through the stress of transitioning to a new stage of life. We learned how to work out together, and simply enjoy each other's company when we went on walks together. When we would bicker, Donovan was always the first to say, "I was wrong, I'm sorry baby." He never let me stay mad at him even if I was wrong. The scripture says in Ephesians 4:26 in the King James Version "Be ye angry, and sin not: let not the sun go down upon your wrath." He truly understood the meaning of not letting the sun set on your wrath.

After I settled in to my apartment, Donovan started to struggle with losing and finding jobs. Sometimes he got discouraged, because his jobs would lay him off at the most inconvenient times, for example, around Christmas. He was such a giving person that he hated the fact that he couldn't spoil me the way that he wanted to spoil me. Gifts and restaurants didn't mean that much to me. I only wanted to spend quality time with him, even if we didn't go out on many dates.

In spite of Donovan's financial hardships, he still managed to throw me my first surprise birthday party. It was one of my best birthdays ever, but it didn't start off that way. First, Donovan told me that he was taking me out to dinner and the movies. I happened to be over at Donovan's house during this time. He had to run some errands so he left me at his house all day by myself. Donovan then called me to say, "Sorry baby, I have to work at the church tonight to video tape the service, so we are going to have to celebrate your birthday tomorrow." I replied, "What…You promised me! You always work at church; they can't find anyone else to work? I will be waiting at your house until you get here so we can talk about this." Donovan never came back to the house, but we exchanged some very angry text messages with each other. Gentleman, just in case you don't know; you never forget to do something special for your girlfriend or wife on her birthday, because you will be in hot water if you do.

Because Donovan canceled our birthday plans, I had no desire to go anywhere, instead, I was determined to sit around in my pajamas with my hair looking nappy all day. However, later that night my friend, Denna, called me and decided that due to the situation, she would take me out to a Mexican restaurant for my birthday. I was crying on the phone with her because I was upset that

Donovan canceled our plans for my birthday. When Denna arrived she made me get dressed, and comb my hair-which made me feel better about my birthday.

Later on that day, Tania arrived at Donovan's house later to take me to Dave and Busters for my birthday. When we stepped outside the door it started to rain like it always rains on my birthday. I said, "Look, it never fails to rain on my birthday no matter where I live." Tania said, "It's just the blessings of God showering down on you." Tania drove me to Dave and Buster's. While we drove to Dave and Busters my mother called me and I explained to her what Donovan did to me on my birthday. My mother replied, "Well, at least he's working for God." I rushed her off the phone, because I really wasn't trying to hear that at that moment. Then my Dad called me and I told him what happened and he couldn't believe that Donovan didn't do anything for my birthday either. My Dad said, "Uh oh, someone is in trouble." I replied, "Yes, someone is in big trouble when I see him."

Finally arriving at Dave and Busters, Tania and I started to walk to the front doors. To my surprise, guess who I see standing there? Donovan! He was standing near the hostess area, which caused me to stop in my tracks. I put my hands on my hips and said, "What are you doing here?" Donovan smiled and gave me a hug. He said that he already had a table for us. We followed him to the table and I saw everyone holding up their menus over their faces. When I came around the corner, they shouted, "Surprise!" I couldn't stop smiling and laughing. Donovan had really surprised me, and I couldn't believe it because I'm hard to surprise. I went around the table and gave everyone a hug. Donovan's Grandparents were there, his parents, friends from the church; friends from my college, my stepmother and my father were all there. I was speechless to say the least.

My friends, Donovan's parents, and Donovan all gave me several gifts. He brought two delicious cakes that had white and pink icing on them. The best gift of all is that Donovan gave me the memory of having my first surprise birthday party; we played games at Dave and Buster and shared many laughs. Tania and Denna were in on the surprise too! Tania just let me go off in the car the whole way there even though she knew Donovan hadn't stood me up on my birthday. Donovan started showing his family members the text messages that he and I exchanged after he canceled my birthday plans and his family found it quite amusing. They told Donovan that there are two things that you can't forget when you are in a relationship: birthdays and anniversaries. Of course, Donovan didn't get in trouble with me; I gave Donovan several kisses when we made it back to my apartment. It feels good to reminiscent on the past happy memories of Donovan.

While I've been grieving these last couple of months there are the things that keep returning to my memories that we were able to share with each other like my surprise birthday party. I know that every relationship isn't perfect, but we were perfect for each other. You have the power to focus only on the positive happy memories. If you choose to focus on the memories that seem a little less than perfect, then unnecessary guilt can easily creep its way into your life and overwhelm you.

As I've taken this step in my grieving process that has caused me to remember and reflect on the memories that I have, Donovan was here with me for a season and only for that season. I can't question God and ask him, "Why, only for a season?" I'm learning to trust God in spite of my emotions and feelings because I know that some people come only for a season and some people come for a lifetime. We can't control everything in our lives. The sooner that you realize that you don't control everything in your life; the sooner you will learn to enjoy the joyous moments in life. Enjoy each day that you spend with your friends and family, because you never know when it's your last Christmas, or birthday party with them. Learn to celebrate every birthday. Every birthday is significant no matter if you are turning 2, 14, and 24 or if it's your sweet 16. Take pictures when you can to capture the moments that you'll want to remember for forever. No matter how busy you are, always make time for the people God has placed in your life, because time is a gift from God that is always fleeting. Investing any amount of time into someone's life is incredibly valuable. Time is not something that can be given back or taken away once given. It is one of the few ways that you can leave a mark on someone else's life- you share a part of you that you can never get back.

You can't be afraid to take risks with love. I'm sure that it was hard for Donovan to ask me to be his girlfriend and it was equally hard for me to open the door to give him the opportunity to ask me. I've been hurt in the past by men, and I wasn't sure what type of man Donovan was going to be because I've had men that seemed like Christians, but had ulterior motives. For example, I've had men tell me that they were celibate but later made advances towards me. Donovan turned out to have the purest soul that I've ever met. If I was afraid to talk to Donovan, then I wouldn't have ever found out that he was incredible.

When you lose someone you love going through the different stages of grief is far more difficult than you could ever imagine. One stage in your grieving process might cause you to remember the happy memories that you shared with that person. Although I was frustrated and unable to comprehend why these memories kept popping up, God revealed to me that you never really lose someone when they pass, because the memories of that person keep them alive in your heart and spirit. I would like to encourage you to sit and think about the memories that you shared with your love one(s).

IF I NEVER

If I never cried, then I would have never known how you can make me smile.
If I never had a broken heart, then I would have never known how you can amend my heart to love again.
If I never lost, I would have never known how it feels to win.
If I never grieved, then I would have never known how time heals all wounds.
If I never was lonely, then I would have never known how you can bring me comfort.
If I never tried, then I would have never known that I can succeed.
If I never made a mistake, then I would have never known that God can forgive me of any sins.
If I never praised God through the storms, then I would have never known that all storms are made to pass.
If I never dreamed, then I would have never known that the sky is the limit.
If I never failed a test, then I would have never known that God gives me re-takes on failed tests.
If I never suffered, then I would have never known that longsuffering is a virtue from God.
If I never said hello to you, then I would have never known that you were a best friend sent from God.

If I never waited for you, then I would have never known patience.

If I never disagreed with you, then I would have never known that conflict brings resolution and resolution builds stronger bonds.

If I never loved, then I would have never known how it feels to love someone unconditionally.

If I never was confused, then I would have never known how to trust God.

If I never invited you into my heart, then I would have never known that God can fill my empty voids.

CHAPTER THREE

THE PHONE CALL FROM HEAVEN

On a Tuesday night in July following Donavan's passing, I had a dream about him. I was in this house with my family members and my Mom was getting a birthday party together. The phone rang and Donovan was calling to speak to me. As I walked to the bedroom with the phone I noticed that Donovan was lying on the bed. I laid my head on his chest as we continued to talk. I told him that I missed him so much and I asked Donovan why he waited so long to contact me? I told Donovan that I wasn't sure what to do in my life. He told me to, "Let him go and move on with my life." I defensively replied, "I don't want to let you go." Donovan said, "I will always be here for you and don't worry about me; do you have a friend?" I disregarded his question and asked him, "What's it like in heaven? Tell me more about how you are doing. What happens when you die? I know you probably can't tell me some things, but I just miss you and I don't know what to do."

Before he could answer any questions I was miraculously back in the kitchen with my mother and Donovan had disappeared from the bedroom. She told me that Marcus, my older brother was on the other line and needed directions to the house. I gave the phone to my Mom and told her not to hang up because Donovan was on the other line. My mom gave Marcus directions and I went to my room to see if Donovan had come back to the bedroom. I went back into the kitchen and I asked my mother for the phone so I could continue talking to Donovan. My mother had hung up the phone. I went to the caller ID to get the number, but the number was unavailable like a bill collector number. I began to cry and I yelled at Mom and asked her, "How could you do that?" I walked back to my room sad and annoyed that my mom had ruined my chance to speak with Donovan.

After the dream, I woke up and began to pray and worship God with the hope of divinely speaking to Donovan. I cried all afternoon missing

Donovan while looking at some pictures. Wanting marriage and children were far away in my mind. I could not see how I could someday love again like I loved Donovan. I realized that unlike in my dream I could not just call Donovan on the phone. I wanted to speak to Donovan in the natural so bad, but sadly I realized that it is only through the spirit I could speak to Donovan.

While in prayer that afternoon my memory was taken back to the night when Donovan received the gift of the Holy Spirit with the evidence of speaking in unknown tongues. If you are unfamiliar with what speaking in unknown tongues means I'm referring to a gift that was received on the day of Pentecost in Acts chapter 2. The apostles were being baptized in the Holy Spirit, which empowered them to proclaim the gospel. Speaking in unknown tongues is a type of gift from God. It is a type of utterance that you make with your mouth, but you don't have control over what you are saying. Your inner spirit is essentially speaking directly to God by praying for things that you may not be aware of, such as current events around the world. If you don't speak in unknown tongues it doesn't mean that the Holy Spirit is not with you, because in Romans chapter 8, the bible teaches us that all believers in Christ have the Holy Spirit that lives within them. When I think back through our time together, Donovan and I made a lot of spiritual growth together. After taking the "Foundations in Christianity" class at my church, I received the gift of the Holy Spirit with the evidence of speaking in tongues. Donovan was saddened because he did not begin speaking in tongues that night. However, only a month later we prayed together at my apartment and he received the gift of the Holy Spirit with the evidence of speaking in tongues! Donovan was so excited to be taken to another place in God. I was thankful to God for allowing me to witness his spiritual growth.

In life it's easy to become convinced that some people are here for a lifetime rather than a season and when God takes them away, for example in a break up, we are left with so many unanswered questions, confusion, and even anger. Most people didn't know that Donovan and I broke up three weeks prior to the accident. Donovan and I had a huge falling out before the accident, which ultimately ended our relationship. In my mind, I somehow knew that we would be able to get passed the situation and at least continue being best friends, but it did not happen that way. Following his death I never understood why things ended the way they did.

About three weeks prior to the accident I had a dream that I was at in a parking lot. My car was parked on top of an enormous hill and I walked all the way to the top of the hill. After reaching the top I was holding onto a large hand as I ran down the hill. After several days of praying about this dream, I received the revelation that I was holding the hand of God. God was telling me that he had taken me up the hill and he would be taking me down the hill. I knew that I had to keep running for the Lord, because He had anointed my feet to run. No matter what the circumstances look like, I must keep running for the Lord.

God was already preparing me for the hard journey that He knew I would have to face in just three weeks. God was telling me that He had my hand and He was never going to leave me nor forsake me. God encouraged me to keep on going no matter what the circumstances looked like on the outside. Although Donovan wasn't going to be in my life I still had to trust God and finish my life's journey.

When God revealed his plan for me to start a Christian boarding school I said to myself, "Wow, God that's a big vision; I know I can't do that alone." I shared God's vision with Donovan and he was making steps towards helping me with God's vision. Donovan was determined that if he was going to be in my life, he was certainly going to help me with God's vision.

I encouraged Donovan to go back to school, because he was hesitant at first without the support of his family. Donovan was much smarter than what most people thought. He was excellent with numbers and history. Despite not knowing that it wasn't God's purpose, Donovan was still making moves towards the righteousness of God. He was always known as a great servant of God. He was always at church when they needed him there to cover the camera, and sometimes it would frustrate me because he wouldn't get the opportunity to enjoy the service with me. The point is, if you're not sure what your plan and purpose is in God, then start making moves towards being a servant to God. Bumps on logs can't move towards God's purpose. Faith without works is dead. You can believe God to do a lot of stuff in your life, but if you don't put some action into it, then how can God do anything for you? Things don't just magically happen for you just because you prayed for them to happen.

      Even if you are still struggling to understand the will of God and know your purpose in life, then you can rest assured that we all have one mission in life. That mission is to go into all nations and preach the gospel of Christ so that all may be saved. Donovan was truly a witness to those he came in contact with. Donovan would be the first and sometimes the only one willing to look crazy as he witnessed to young brothers in Christ about abstaining from sex until marriage. Donovan truly lived out what he believed, because we were waiting for marriage until we had sex. We dated for three and a half years, and he never attempted to pressure me into having sex. I was ready to get married, but now I've realized that I must continue to wait even longer. My mother always told me that good things come to those who wait and I'm learning to take her advice in my life as I continue to wait on God. Donovan stood firm on his faith and was never afraid to share the gospel to anyone.

Although Donovan may have been called weird or different, he didn't care because what he was doing was for the Lord. This made me wonder, in the end of your life, when you are on your deathbed (if you are fortunate to make it there), what will matter? Will it matter that you fit in with the crowds? Will it matter that you had a lot of friends? No, it won't matter in the end. The only thing that will matter is what you did for God in the allotted time that you've been given. God has appointed unto man one time to be born and one time to die. You may not get the chance to die of old age, because some of you will be taken unexpectedly like my dear friend Donovan. What will you say to God if you never serve him? What will be your response if God asks you "Why were you ashamed of me?" Just to think about God asking me a question like that gives me chills. Don't be afraid to speak to people about Jesus, because they do not have a heaven or hell to put you in. Share the gospel and your testimony, because it can make a difference in someone's life.

As I sit here, I wonder what would I really say to Donovan if I could get a phone call to heaven? What would he tell me? I would probably start the conservation by asking how he's doing. I would then proceed to ask what it's like in heaven? Do you miss me? I would confess how much I miss him and still love him, regardless of what happened between us. I would want him to tell me if he's watching over me, if this pain will ever go away, and if I will ever be able to move on and find a new love, or am I destined to be alone? I couldn't tell you how many times I've asked myself these questions thinking Donovan would be able to hear me and respond to me.

Some people call me a loner because of the time I've been spending alone since Donovan's passing, but I know that God has used this time to teach me. Truthfully, I'm not a loner, but in this time I have been learning that sometimes God will isolate you to bring revelation to you. God has taught me patience, love, and longsuffering. I've also learned to love people in spite of them mistreating me. Although the relationship Donovan and I shared wasn't perfect, I still loved Donovan all the way to the end. When we were broken up during his last three weeks I still loved

Donovan. To this day I will never stop loving him. Donovan was my best friend, and my companion. I learned how to love someone unconditionally despite their flaws. This type of love mimics the way that God loves us. God loves us in spite of our shortcomings, sins, and disobedience. God chooses to love us even when we don't spend time with him or make him a priority in our lives. My relationship with Donovan also taught me longsuffering. I'm continuing to learn about longsuffering, but I'm just curious as to how long I will have to suffer with this loneliness? How long will it be before I'm blissfully happy again? How long God? Well, I've learned to stop asking God those questions and I've learned to be content with my life.

I'm content with my life because God is supplying all of my needs. I have health in my body, I have eyes to see, ears to hear, legs to walk, a tongue to speak, family members, Godly friends, a church home, a car, a home for shelter, clothes on my back, food to eat, my youth, purpose, destiny, hope, faith, dreams, visions, money, and a bountiful more things that would take chapters to list. I'm still here and I have purpose in my life. I know that what I'm going through is not for me- it's for someone else. My life is a testimony and I must share what God has done for me with the world! My testimony can help someone else who loses a love one and doesn't know how to deal with life and their emotions. I have to remember that I told God "Yes, I will serve you. Yes, I will do your will no matter what I have to sacrifice. It doesn't matter who you have to take out of my life." I still stand resolved and I declare that I will continue the good fight of faith and my heart, my soul, my mind, and my spirit will still say yes to God. I will write a book if that's what you want me to do. I will write poetry. I will go around the world and speak of your glory. I will encourage others. I will speak blessings and not cursing into others' lives.

Always remember, when you say yes to God; you better be careful, because your yes can mean that you might have to go through some suffering. God never said that this life would be easy. If Jesus suffered while he was on earth and I'm a disciple of Jesus Christ, why wouldn't I have to suffer? We all have our own crosses to bare in life.

When you truly say yes to God, then you must get ready for the enemy to start attacking you. The enemy will attack you by using your weaknesses and trying to hinder you from God's purpose. The enemy will use those closest to you to throw darts into your life. For example, the enemy could use your spouse, your children, your parents, or your best friend to stir up trouble in your life. The enemy is not afraid of your past, but is fearful of the potential of your future. The enemy only goes after valuable things. If you had no value in your life, then the enemy will not bother you. If the enemy is constantly attacking you, then start praising God for the value that He has put in your life.

In the same way that any other being has weaknesses- I too struggle with weaknesses. First of all, I'm human and that means I have flesh. We live in the natural world so therefore, we have natural desires like sex. I don't want to be lonely so I long to have people- whether they are the right people or the wrong people- in my life to fill the void of loneliness even when I know that they are not part of my destiny. That's a hindrance in my life and I recognize this. It is crucial to be able to recognize weaknesses in your life in order to be prepared for the enemy's tactics. I've been waiting patiently on the Lord for my husband and sometimes I get anxious, but that's a weakness that I must be aware of at all times. I'm not giving up on God, because God has already showed me in a dream that I will walk down the aisle and get married someday. I won't allow the enemy to talk to me and discourage me simply because I don't have a potential husband in my life. It's hard to accept this and continue waiting patiently, when it seems as though everyone around me is getting married. Even though the wait is hard, I'm becoming increasing stronger and patient because

I refuse to get married to someone who is not part of my destiny.

Waiting on God is not always easy, but it's necessary. I don't want a lifetime of headaches and regrets from a decision that I rushed to make because I got tired of waiting on God to supply me with an answer. I'm tired of asking these questions to God: How long I will have to suffer with this loneliness? How long will it be before I'm blissfully happy again? How long God? I've come to the sad realization that Donovan isn't coming back and he's not going to answer my questions. God is not going to answer my questions when I want them answered and how I want them answered. What to do with myself now? The only thing I can do is to live life for God. Donovan is gone forever and the only chance that I will have to see him again is in heaven. There's a saying that says "Time heals all wounds." Well, I'm waiting for my wounds to heal. In the meantime I don't know if I will ever be able to function normally again. It's been seven months and I can't see past getting over Donovan. You know I sometimes visualize what Donovan would have said to me before he died. This is what God gave me…

IF I DIE

If I die tomorrow, will you know how I feel?
Will you know that if I died tomorrow, I'm glad that I knew you today?
If I died tomorrow, I would have no regrets about you, or my life.
If I died tomorrow, I would become an angel and guard you through your life.
I will always be there to help you in the time of need.
Although I would be angry that I could not share with you some of the joys of this world, I would still be happy for you.
When it's your turn to go I will ask God if I can come down to get you to bring to heaven. If God says yes, I will help you fly away with me to home.

CHAPTER FOUR

DONOVAN, THE TEACHER

Some people are natural born leaders, and others must learn how to become leaders over time. In the same way, some people are natural born teachers. However, others must learn how to become teachers over time. Donovan was a natural born teacher and he taught many people how to live a Godly life. I was a student of Donovan's teaching and a few of the things he taught me include:
1. Laugh shamelessly
2. Eat plenty
3. Give wet kisses
4. Forgive quickly

5. Don't let the sun set on your wrath

Donovan had a contagious laugh that could brighten up a room and make you laugh even if you didn't know what was funny. He was full of the joy of God and he truly knew how to smile through the storms of life. His laughter served as his witness tool to how good God was in his life in spite of trials and tribulations. Although the devil attempted to steal his joy by discouraging him through seemingly impossible to overcome trials such as job loss, he always knew how to laugh his way through the tough times. This joy resulted in his ability to rest in God knowing everything would work out.

Donovan had a huge appetite for all kinds of food. He didn't have a favorite food, because he loved all kinds of foods. I could always tell if he liked the food he was eating, because he would eat his food as if he thought someone was going to steal it if he didn't eat it quickly! If he didn't like the food then he would force himself to eat all the food, but he would eat it unnaturally slow. If I didn't like my food I would give the rest of my food to him, and he would reply "I'm not a garbage disposer," but that didn't stop him from eating my food. Every meal for Donovan was eaten with pleasure, which was a testament to his ever-present gratefulness for the often undervalued treasures in life.

Donovan wasn't afraid to show his love for others by giving them wet kisses. His wet kisses would drive me crazy. It's almost as if he would have slobber on his lips as he came to give you a kiss on the cheek or lips. Donovan's sisters would push him away when he tried to give them wet kisses. Although the wet kisses drove me crazy I secretly didn't mind them. What wouldn't I give if I could have a wet kiss from him today? It's the little awkward things that we learn to love about someone and miss whenever they are gone.

Donovan had the most forgiving spirit that I've ever seen. He would forgive anyone that wronged him, and would never hold a grudge. He had the sweetest spirit that I have ever met. If one of his family members ever mistreated him and yelled at him his reply was always, "It's okay, they didn't mean it. I forgive them anyway." If I ever did anything wrong he would always say, "It's okay; we are not perfect." It amazed me how someone could be so quick to forgive. He never stayed mad at me. Nor did he let me stay mad at him. Donovan truly understood the Godly principal of never letting the sun set on your wrath. If I was mad at him for something he quickly would say, "I'm sorry, I was wrong, please forgive me." How could you not forgive someone who would first admit that they were wrong and then ask for your forgiveness? I could never stay mad at him and sometimes it drove me crazy, but I appreciated the lesson that he showed me. If you are mad at your significant other ask yourself, "Will this matter a year from now?" If the answer is no, then it's probably not worth being mad about. Here are the next five lessons that Donovan taught me:

1. Dance even if you don't know how to dance
2. Love without conditions
3. Enjoy all kinds of music
4. Be sweet to everyone you meet
5. Live life to the fullest without caring what anyone thinks of you

Donovan did not have any rhythm, but he loved to dance. It made me laugh when he danced because he looked like he was having so much fun dancing off beat. He didn't care if people looked at him and laughed even if he couldn't dance. I used to try to help him learn how to dance on beat, but sometimes it proved to be useless, because he would go right back to dancing off beat. Then I would say, "Forget it" and just let him dance to his own beat. I loved the fact that he would dance even if I laughed at him. Donovan's illustrated his freedom in being himself just like the William Purkey's quote, "You've gotta dance like there's nobody watching, love like you'll never be hurt, sing like there's nobody listening, and live like it's heaven on earth." Donovan taught me to dance as if you are the only person in the room. I'm not sure if David danced like this in the bible, but the bible talks about how David danced with all of his might before the Lord. There's nothing wrong with releasing stress by dancing as long as you are not sending images that are not honoring your body or if you are sending promiscuous messages to the opposite sex. I hope that you get the chance to dance in life.

  Donovan was my teacher when it came to the meaning of love; a word that encompasses a multitude of meanings. He taught me that to love someone means that you must be willing to make sacrifices. He made numerous sacrifices for me. He supported me when I moved into my first apartment, and when I moved into my house. Even if he wasn't working he had a savings account that he was willing to use to support me financially through the times he was not working. He showed me love every time we went on a walk together, every time he bragged about me to his family, every time we went on a date, every time he suffered with me when I didn't have any air conditioning in my house, and every time I didn't have any heat in my house. There was even a time that I threw up at his grandmother's house all over her carpet and hard wood floors. Donovan cleaned up my mess and took me to his house and took care of me as I continued to throw up all over his bathroom floors. If no one else had my back I knew I had his support in everything. He gave me money to take my test to get my teacher's certification. Most men would not be willing to do many of the things that he did for me to only receive love in return. Most men would want sex, but he was a true gentleman. I just knew he would someday become my husband.

    Donovan taught me how to enjoy all kinds of music. He loved listening to contemporary Christian and gospel music. His favorite artist was Toby Mac. Since Donovan was a young black man in society, some people and family members criticized his taste in music, but that didn't stop him. When I was younger my family members laughed at me because I loved listening to the white contemporary Christian groups. As a result, I stopped listening to the white contemporary Christian groups and only listened to the black gospel artists. After meeting Donovan, he freed me from feeling ashamed of the fact that I enjoy listening to white contemporary Christian groups. He was comfortable being himself, which inspired me to be myself. Now, you will find me listening to all kinds of Christian artists. The color of your skin doesn't matter as long as you are singing about Jesus.

Donovan taught me to be sweet to everyone you meet because you could be entertaining an angel. There was this strange man at church that stared and followed him all around the church. Donovan wouldn't mind being followed by this guy, but other church members didn't give the strange man the time of day. This strange man would wait until all the church buses were gone to ask him for a ride in his car. He would give this man a ride in his car, which is a lot more than what most people would do for this strange man, but Donovan was different because he had a kind and giving heart. After everyone found out about the accident there were so many people that I didn't know he knew from going to grocery stores, banks, work, school, and church that showed up for his funeral. He was sweet to everyone he met. He could talk your ear off if you let him. My mother would spend hours on the phone talking to Donovan about the message in church, or what was going on in his life. It always made me smile, because Donovan would be so satisfied and happy to be sharing what he learned with someone else.

Donovan lived his life to the fullest without caring what anyone thought of him. He enjoyed serving God at church through video ministry,

working with different companies, going back to school, reading his bible, and having fun with me. It didn't bother him that some of his family didn't support the idea that he wanted to go back to school to get a bachelor's degree. It didn't bother him if people in his family didn't approve of him having me as his girlfriend. Donovan was going to live his life to the fullest. He had truly begun making his own decisions and growing up into the man of God that he was called to be. He couldn't care less about what anyone else thought about our relationship, or what he was doing in life. I was proud of the progress that he made in the short three in a half years that I watched him grow up into the man God wanted him to be. He encouraged me to be myself no matter what anyone thought of me. Donovan was also my instructor for the following lessons:
1. Be humble
2. Be a faithful servant
3. You will never find perfection, but there is someone perfect for you
4. Celebrate every birthday no matter if you think they are significant years or not
5. Fold your clothes until they are creased like you ironed them

 Being a humble person means that you are not prideful or arrogant. Donovan had the opportunity to meet celebrities during his video projects, but he never boasted about meeting them. He had a meek and humble heart that was teachable. If he was ever wrong about anything, he would listen to the voice of reason without back talking. Donovan could take criticism without taking offense to anything.

With any work that you do for the Lord you must be a faithful servant unto God. Donovan was a good example of this because he was faithful by volunteering at church almost every Thursday night service and Sunday service. Sometimes I would say, Donovan why can't someone else serve this Sunday so you can sit and worship with me. He would simply say, "They need me." Donovan had a servant's heart just as Jesus serves us. Jesus demonstrated a servant's heart in many of the recorded stories in the bible. Jesus is the Good Shepherd just as St. John 10:11 tells us. "I am the good shepherd. The good shepherd gives His life for the sheep" which is what Christ did for all sinners.

Donovan taught me that you will never find perfection, but there is someone perfect for you. When I first met him I just knew he was perfect and never made a mistake. He told me that he wasn't perfect, because he made some poor decisions. During this particular season in our lives, we were perfect for each other. At the time,

I didn't know that our season wasn't going to last for a lifetime. Donovan would say, "If anything ever happens between us, remember the next person you date won't be perfect either, but you would have to accept their flaws too." Those words stuck with me, because I was able to see the flaws in Donovan over time, but I loved him in spite of the flaws. Loving someone in spite of his or her flaws is called unconditional love. We were perfect for each other, because we grew spiritually together. We helped each other grow towards what God called us to be at that particular time in our lives.

As we learned each other's personalities, we also learned how to celebrate each other. As you already know from previous chapters, Donovan was the first person to throw me a surprise birthday party. I threw him a surprise birthday party for his 24th birthday. To some, turning 24 years old may not seem incredibly significant. It's not like someone turning 16 and being able to drive, or turning 21 and being legal to drink alcohol-there is no specific privilege associated with turning 24. I didn't care that it didn't seem like a significant number for his birthday; I was only concerned that Donovan felt special on his birthday because he made me feel special on my birthday. I was glad that I threw Donovan a surprise birthday because he didn't make it to his 25th birthday.

    I threw his birthday party a week before his real birthday. I decorated his basement with Mexican themed items and a piñata that he tried to break. There was Mexican food, gifts, music, games, family, friends, and smiles. I blindfolded Donovan as I drove from my house to his house. I told him we were going out to eat to celebrate him getting a job. I walked him to his back door. When I took the blindfold off his eyes, everyone shouted "Surprise!" Donovan was so surprised and excited. All I could remember was his smile. Donovan smiled so much that night. I was excited that he was surprised and happy. It made me happy that I could make him feel special. He told me that no one ever threw him a surprise birthday party before so I was glad to be the first to treat him special on his birthday.

    Even after the party, I felt that I was able to give him a gift far better than tactile presents and food. I was able to help God create a wonderful memory for Donovan and his family. For his last birthday he had fun and he felt special. Friends and family were there and he felt loved by everyone. I have many pictures to remember that moment. I encourage everyone to always celebrate birthdays because you never know when your last birthday will be, or when the last time you will get to celebrate with family and friends.

    In every picture and memory that I have of Donovan, he was always clean cut and neat. After knowing Donovan, I cultivated an attitude to always look your best no matter the day. He would fold his clothes until they were creased like he ironed them. He would spend hours doing laundry, because he folded every piece of clothing neatly. I would just watch him in awe, because I never had patience to fold clothes with that much care. I could fold a basket of clothes within five minutes. He could pack many clothes in a suitcase because every article of clothing was neatly packed. Donovan would go as far as to create space between his clothes in his closet using his fingers. Sometimes I would run my fingers through his closet just to annoy him by throwing the spacing off. Donovan would get this irritated look on his face, but it made me smile. He had pride in the way that he looked. From my memory, even the last time that I saw Donovan, he was clean cut. It was his Saturday routine to either get a line up or haircut. I was proud of the way that he always looked. When I see Donovan in my head, I see that bright smile, neat clothes, and hear his joyous laughter. I know that he is at peace and happy. I miss my best friend, but I know that we will one day see each other again. Donovan coached me on the following lessons:

1. Enjoy sweet treats
2. Be a hard worker
3. Strive for goals
4. Persevere despite negative opinions about your future
5. Give gifts to someone you love to show them you appreciate them

Donovan loved to eat sweet treats. He loved cakes, ice-cream, pudding, and cookies. I would get onto him about not eating too many sweets, but he would still eat them. We both were guilty for indulging in guilty pleasures. He would say, "I will still love you even if you gain a little weight." Every time he would say that I would just feel more comfortable with eating more sweets. Donovan enjoyed eating all kinds of foods, but he really loved eating sweets. His parents also warned him not to eat too many sweets because diabetes runs in his family. He would always come over to my house, because I was lenient with allowing him to eat whatever he wanted. I'm glad Donovan was able to enjoy different kinds of foods while he was on this earth. Although too much of anything in life isn't good for you, allowing yourself to indulge every once in a while is okay.

Donovan's life taught me how to be a hard worker to achieve any goals. It is unrealistic for one to wake up one day and pray that a job falls out of sky if you haven't applied for one. It is foolish for anyone to believe they can become smarter or wiser without opening a book and studying. Donovan taught me that you must strive for any goals that you set forth in your life. Each day that you are alive, you must take steps towards you goals. Whether they are baby steps, or leaps of faith, it doesn't matter you must learn to just "Go." For example, Donovan had a goal to go back to school and get a higher degree after being out of school for a couple of years. Despite criticism from his friends and family, he went back to school and worked hard towards his goal.

I find myself asking this question, "If I knew my last day was tomorrow, would I still work hard towards my goals today?" The answer to that question is yes. Although tomorrow is not promised it doesn't give anyone an excuse to remain stagnant. I also wonder, "If I die tomorrow, will my work go in vain?" The answer to that question is a resounding no. Each day that you live your life to the fullest, someone is watching you. You are someone's role model even though you can't always see him or her. When you die, what do you want people to remember you by? Do you want them to say, "She tried to change the world" or maybe "She changed my world, because I was motivated by her tenacity?" Well, Donovan changed my world and motivated me by his tenacity. He was a person not willing to give up no matter what obstacles life decided to throw at him. Sometimes he needed a little push, as all of us do at some point or another, but he was not giving up. He was a true servant of God, which was evident in his hard working mentality that he brought with him in many areas of his life.

Donovan persevered despite negative opinions regarding his future. Although he was questioned about why he was going back to school he went anyway. One of the saddest days I remembered was when Donovan came to my house with tears in his eyes, because someone told him that he needs to just be a truck driver because it's a job that he can grasp quickly. Donovan was sad by the comment, but I motivated him to strive for his goals in spite of the negative comments. Granted there's nothing wrong with being a truck driver, but when someone says, "I want to be a doctor" do you reply, "Why, you should just learn to bag groceries because it's easier?" Wow, talk about self-esteem buster. One should never shoot anyone's dreams down even if you think they will struggle with achieving those goals. Without failures in life, then there could be no success. Donovan pressed through the negative opinions and started to work towards his goals.

A more uplifting goal I learned from Donovan is to give gifts to someone you love to show them that you appreciate them. Donovan surprised me on more than one occasion with pink flowers on my birthday and at my job. Once he surprised me at my job with flowers, and when I asked him why? He simply replied, "Just because." All day my smile was from ear to ear because he thought about me and gave me pink flowers. Pink is my favorite color. On one of my birthdays he surprised me with a dozen pink roses, which was the sweetest surprise when I woke up at his house. If you have never woken up to the smell of pink roses, then you have yet to experience one of God's sweet aromas. Learn to give gifts to someone you love just because, and not because you are fighting, or for birthday celebrations. Just learn to show the person you love that you love them just because God gave you the chance to create memories with that person. I cherish every memory God allowed for Donovan and me to share. Memories are one of the greatest gifts in the world.

The next five lessons I learned…
1. Adore your significant other

2. Imagine that your significant other is the only one for you and treat him or her that way
3. Encourage others
4. Patience
5. Smile brightly even if your teeth aren't perfect

Adoration is an uncommon word that people don't use in daily life. As Christians we use the term adoration when we speak in reference to adoring God, which means paying honor to God. Often times we forget how to show the person we love that we appreciate them. Just as you adore God simply because of whom He is; you should learn how to adore your significant other simply because of who they are. Your relationship with your heavenly father should be the model of how you show love to others, which includes your significant other.

Donovan used almost every opportunity to show his love to me in some form of fashion. Whether it was simply spending quality time by rubbing my back in the most innocent way, or cooking dinner for me, he was willing to let his guards down to show me that he appreciated and loved me. I showed Donovan that I adored him as well by the constant praises that I gave him to encourage his positive traits. I adored him when I cooked for him in spite of being tired, or when I rubbed his head and massaged his shoulders.

God is an excellent example of the way you should show love to your mate. God provides provisions for us. God doesn't complain when He does things for us even when we are undeserving. God gave His only begotten son "Jesus" for our sins so that we may have eternal life. God is worthy of praise and adoration. Sometimes I wonder how God feels when His people don't praise and worship him. Many people don't acknowledge God for all the provisions He gives us. Some don't spend any quality time with Him, except for in a prayer before a meal. How do you think God feels when we don't spend much time with Him? What if the shoes were on the other foot, how would you feel if your significant other didn't spend much time with you? My relationship with Donovan helped me to realize that my relationship with God had to grow and be stronger. God is a jealous God. It's like God saying how dare you adore another human being first, without adoring me for who I am?

I imagined that Donovan was the only person for me and I tried to treat him that way. When I was with him, I couldn't see myself marrying anyone else. With my words I tried to reaffirm him that I was in the relationship all the way. Donovan would tell me that I was the one for him and he couldn't see anyone else with me. He showed me that he loved me and he tried to treat me that way. The only way that you can treat your significant other the right way is with God's help. If you fall off track, or lack God in your life, then you are bound to mistreat your significant other. You must always stay close to God. Your relationship with God is the foundation for a healthy, faithful, and loving relationship. When you understand how God loves, then you understand how you should love. God wants the very best for His children. We are all God's children; therefore, we should all be treated like royalty. God is the King of Kings, and Lord of Lords. God is the ruler of the universe, and if we belong to Him, then we deserve to be treated the very best.

Donovan and I learned how to encourage each other and how to be patient. We learned each other's fears and cried with each other when we were hurt. We felt each other's pain and learned how to pacify each other. When Donovan kept losing his jobs, I was always there saying "We will be ok. We don't have to go on a date every week. We can just spend time together at the house." Donovan would get discouraged because he was trying to save up for a ring, but he felt that he kept getting set back with every job lost. I always told myself, "What if that was me, what would I want him to do for me?" I would want him to encourage me and not put me off to the side. When I was down because it was hard finding a teaching job, or a place to live Donovan was always there cheering me on. You have to have someone in your corner besides your Mom. Your Mom will always encourage you, but sometimes it seems more impactful to have someone else say encouraging words to you.

Others can typically see skills and gifts on the inside of you, even when you can't see them. Sometimes just speaking encouraging words to others is all the motivation they need to keep on going. You never know what a person is going through until you walk in their shoes. It doesn't hurt you, or take any value away from you when you speak words of kindness to others. As a teacher in the public school system, I had to learn how to speak words of kindness even when I didn't want to speak kind words. Sometimes it only takes a smile or a hug to encourage others. Donovan was good at giving kisses, and hugs to everyone. If you were having a bad day, then you could trust and believe that he would surely give you a hug to brighten up your day.

Donovan was a patient man when it came to many things in life. He waited for a true girlfriend that cared for him, which was me. He was waiting for marriage before engaging in sex. He was constantly waiting for a job that he desired. He learned how to stop complaining about his present situation through patience. When I first met Donovan I taught him how to be grateful for the blessings that he already had in his life. He learned to thank God for his car, because some people didn't even have a car. He learned to thank God for only having a phone and car insurance bill, while others had almost 8 bills every month. Patience taught him that life happens, money comes and money goes. He soon learned that complaining wouldn't help resolve any problems

Patience is a virtue, and Donovan definitely had patience. He taught me how to wait on things like furniture. When I moved into a house from an apartment, my house was not fully furnished. Donovan taught me that it's ok not to have everything at first. He taught me to pay off furniture before trying to use credit cards to buy furniture. Donovan taught me many of life's principles that I hadn't previously learned on my own.

I learned to smile brightly even if my teeth weren't perfect. Donovan would tell me that he wanted to get his teeth fixed because he had an under bite. I would tell him not to worry about it, because we would fix it when we got married and had more money. Donovan's under bite never stopped him from smiling. He had this smile that could brighten up a room, and a contagious laugh that would make me laugh. I loved the fact that Donovan could smile and laugh through the insecurity of his under bite. It never stopped him from having joy in his spirit. Sometimes I just look at his pictures to see his smile, because it always makes me smile. Then I can always hear his laughter. Even as I'm writing this down, I hear his laughter in my spirit. Donovan's spirit will live on in my heart, because I carry him there daily. I'm sure those who knew Donovan can hear his laughter as you read this book.

I believe that every relationship that we have is for a purpose, because you learn from other people. You have to open up your heart and your mind to allow them to teach you. As you can see Donovan taught me very valuable life lessons that I use every day. My relationship with Donovan has made me a better person. I challenge you to think about the different relationships in your life, such as, friendships, significant others, co-workers, and even your siblings and think on the lessons they have taught you. As you begin to think about the different lessons you will find that every person that has been in your life has contributed to the person that you are today. I am eternally grateful to God for allowing Donovan into my life even if it was just for a season. I'm thankful to Donovan for being comfortable with yourself and letting your light shine in my life.

TEACH ME

Teach me patience.
Teach me how to pray.
Teach me to appreciate life.
Teach me to give wet kisses.
Teach me how to celebrate life.
Teach me how to not stay angry.
Teach me how to study your word.
Teach me how to encourage others.
Teach me how to let go of the baggage.
Teach me how to laugh through the storms.
Teach me how to desire the things that you desire.
Teach me to build others up, instead of tear others down.
Teach me how to dance like I'm the only one in the room.
Teach me how to be a humble and faithful servant unto you God.
Teach me to how to be content no matter what my life looks like.
Teach me how to not wait until someone is gone to give pink flowers.
Teach me how to persevere for my goals in spite of negative opinions.
Last, but certainly not least, teach me how to love like God loves mankind.

CHAPTER FIVE

WATCH OUT FOR HINDRANCES

The grieving process lends itself to several hindrances. Keep in mind that you are still on this earth for God's plan and purpose. You can't let the enemy distract you with hindrances while you are in the grieving process. One thing is certain- when you lose a significant other or spouse in your life you will have a need to feel touched and loved by someone to fill the void of the one you've lost in your life. This is when the enemy will send everything that looks like gold your way, or it could even look like grass. Even if it looks like grass you don't care, because you want someone to hold you to calm your fears.

As I started the process of grieving; males from my past started to re-surface. The males from my past presented themselves as wanting to be a friend to me while going through this difficult process. At first, I was accepting of their friendships. There was one male in particular that drew closer to me through this process. He would come over just to hold me close while I cried and screamed in pain of losing Donovan. He started to treat me to dinners and take me to the movies. I didn't realize was happening at the time, but old feelings started to arise on the inside of me.

One thing is for sure, there's always a reason why past relationships didn't work out the first time around. At first, I entertained the thought of this friend coming back into my life because I felt lonely. However, just because you feel lonely doesn't warrant you to date anyone without first asking God if that man or woman is a part of your destiny. Sometimes, when we know someone isn't supposed to remain in our lives for more than a season we ignore that knowledge. Don't worry, this revelation didn't come too late. I allowed this man to come back into my life without even fully realizing what was happening. When he initially presented himself to me he just wanted to be my friend. As time went by and he continued to comfort me through my grief and pain he slowly was beginning to creep back into my life as more than a friend. This will happen all so slyly in your life.

    My friend began to call me on the phone all the time. He started to hold my hand and cuddle with me while we were watching movies. He started to refer to me as "baby." Before I realized it I overheard him on the phone calling me "his girlfriend!" I think that was the moment it hit me. This man just called me his "girlfriend!" All this time I thought I was innocently having this friend around me all the time to comfort me through the grief. Then I began to realize that I was only using him to fill a void in my life that was empty because of my lost. I imagined that he was Donovan. When I closed my eyes while we cuddled on the couch I was imagining that he was Donovan holding me.

    Finally, I came back to reality and realized the reason this man believed I was his girlfriend was because I had been leading him to this conclusion, because I allowed him to creep back into my life without even knowing I did. Then I started to freak out because I knew I hadn't asked God if this was the person for me. I began to think about why we didn't have a long term relationship in the beginning anyway? Can this person actually be my boyfriend?

God quickly began to show me my list of qualities that I wanted out of a husband. When I was a teenager I made a T-chart, and on one side I wrote out the qualities that I wanted out of a husband and the other side I wrote out my non-negotiable qualities. I wanted someone who was humble, faithful, gentle, kind, loving, family man. I wanted my husband to have a go-getter personality, and to be in constant search for God's heart. I wanted to know that my husband was a spiritual leader. Donovan made it very difficult for the next man to come into my life. I began to evaluate my friend to see if he could even stand a chance in being in my life. This man was kind, he had a big heart, loved music, and he was very giving. Unfortunately, he struggled with smoking weed over the years. My friend use to be in the entertainment business, in which he was part of a singing group. He was a handsome man, but there were things that he was struggling with in his life. He was a newborn in the Christian family so I knew I would have to lead the way in the spiritual aspect of our relationship. God was speaking to me by saying, "don't forget the things that you said you wanted out of a relationship." Don't be so quick to love and be loved that you will fall for anyone. God knew that my desire for my husband was to truly be the spiritual headship of our relationship. If I was the stronger Christian, then that would mean that I would be leading him.

Don't get me wrong, this man was attractive, charming, giving, and he had a huge heart, but he was newly finding his way with God. God wanted something different in my life. I was at a vulnerable state of being when this man came back into my life. My friend was an inevitable hindrance towards God's plan and purpose for my life.

Hindrances do not always look dark and gloomy, because my friend was on his way to becoming a better person. A hindrance is anything that impedes or stops you from doing your God-given purpose. God did not have him in his plans for my life. I had to be obedient to what God was speaking to me at the time.

I felt horrible for leading my friend on, and for being selfish by using him as a replacement to fill the void in my life. He was my make-believe Donovan in a sense. I was able to close my eyes and picture that it was Donovan holding my hand and cuddling with me. If I was still speaking to my friend today I would sincerely apologize for using him.

Eventually I had to tell him that he was not part of my destiny. I knew that his feelings had grown stronger towards me over time, and my feelings did too. I had to put my feelings over to the side, because God told me that he wasn't my husband. Sometimes in life we make emotional decisions based on our feelings. I've learned that your feelings are fickle and will fade fast. I had to make a decision that was based on the God factor. I didn't want anything to hinder what God had for me down the road.

Even once you are obedient to God you must still be careful of the enemy's attacks. The enemy will begin to try to send more distractions your way. He will send other males to try to fill the void, but remember the devil doesn't need any new tricks because all his old ones still work. If the devil fooled you before, please don't let him fool you again with the same lesson. The devil will send you someone that looks like gold, but is really brass when you examine them with a microscope. The devil is always at work, but you must be prepared for his tricks. If you know you have a weakness of feeling lonely, then the devil will continue to send Tom, Bob, John, and Steven your way to fill your empty void. The devil will do this in an attempt to make you ignore the voice of God who is trying to tell you "all you need is me right now, and you don't need anyone else but me to fill your void." Once you completely surrender your life to God and make a declaration that you will not make decisions on your own, then you must stand firm on your word. I told God that I didn't want anyone in my life that wasn't part of my destiny, and that's exactly what God honored in my life.

God showed me through my friend's actions that he was not the one for me. God also spoke to me through dreams that I would have a night. Anytime I was involved in a relationship that was not of God, I would have nightmares, which was God's way of showing me to get out of the relationship. You have to learn the ways that God speaks to you. God is always speaking to you, but are you listening? God cannot give you the desires of your heart until you totally and completely submit your life unto Christ. As you submit your life to Christ your desires will become God's desires. When you think you desire Tom and Bob in your life you can simply ask yourself, "Am I in the will of God?" If you are not in the will of God, then of course God will not give you your Tom and Bob for your own good. Later on in life you will be thanking God for not giving you those foolish desires that you thought you wanted. You don't want to feel like you wasted your time or anyone else's time while being in the wrong relationship.

From my life lesson I want you to learn that when you are grieving for your significant other then you must not let hindrances distract you from

God's purpose and plan for your life while you are on earth. I had to realize that I was not dead. I had to continue to live out God's plan and purpose. Remember that God will continue to speak to you in all sorts of methods; you must be willing to listen and heed God's warnings. In this next poem I want to dedicate it to my friend that was there for me through my grieving process. If you ever read this, then please know that I am truly sorry. I pray for God's blessing over your life and that God will give you the desires of your heart. I pray that God will send you your soul mate. Thank you for helping me learn this life lesson.

I'M SORRY

I'm sorry that every time you looked at me I pictured him.
I'm sorry that I compared your every being to him.
I'm sorry that when you eased my pain, your love for me grew.
I'm sorry that I loved you in a different way.
In time I hope that you will find exactly what you want.
In time I hope that you will lead the way spiritually for your wife.
In time I hope that you will forgive me for my selfish ways.
In time I hope that you will understand the ways in which God speaks.
In time I hope you will see just how much you meant to me.
Although you were not part of my destiny, you helped me get to where I am today.
Thank you for sharing your time and love with me for a season.

CHAPTER SIX

THE BREAK UP

Only three weeks before the tragic car accident Donovan and I broke up. It wasn't an easy break up. As I share this part of my life, I pray that you read my words in the spirit that I'm meaning to share them with you. In no way are my intensions to make Donovan look bad, but I want to be completely honest, naked, and unashamed as I share my story so that it will minister to you and give you some wisdom on relationships.

In my eyes, Donovan was every wonderful thing that I wrote about in the first five chapters-a Christian man with a humble and meek spirit, but he was also human. As you know, all humans make mistakes and fall short of God's glory. Even if you think you are with the best Christian man or woman of God, do not be deceived because we are all fleshly beings. Until we become spiritual beings we are all subject to make mistakes and fall into temptation if we do not learn to kill our flesh daily.

    Thinking back on the break up with Donovan there were many signs that God gave me that were warning signs that he was not the one for me. In the last year that we were together, I began to pray to God earnestly to find out if Donovan was my God ordained husband. Little did I know that God was answering my prayer all along through the last year that we were together. God had shown me signs that should have been red flags that there was a problem going on in our relationship. One night we were watching a movie downstairs in the basement. It was getting late and Donovan fell asleep while watching the movie. His cell phone went off late at night and I said to myself "Who could be calling him this late at night?" Naturally I grabbed his phone and looked at the missed call from a girl named Athena. I decided to look through his text messages. I saw a text message to this girl from Donovan about meeting at Red Lobster for dinner. I was shocked and disturbed. His Facebook page was still opened on his laptop, so I decided to do a little more investigating by looking at some of his messages. He sent a message to a girl from high school explaining that he thought she was cute in high school. After seeing the Facebook message and textbook messages, I said to myself "Whoa, has he lost his mind?" I woke Donovan up and exposed the text messages and Facebook message.

Once Donovan was awake he told me he was planning to meet with a girl at Red Lobster to talk about how to propose to me and where to get a good ring. Now mind you this girl was unmarried and I didn't know this chick. I asked Donovan, "Well, why wouldn't you ask a married person like your mom or why wouldn't you ask one of my friends?" Then I said, "Why are you sending messages to this girl talking about you were cute in high school? You have a girlfriend now, and you don't do that!" This was a big argument, but when I talked it over with my mom she told me that Donovan had talked to her about getting advice about the proposal and about the ring. My mom said, "You young girls don't know how to appreciate it when a good man is trying to do something special for you." So I went along with it and forgave Donovan although my suspicions were raised. This was the first red flag that should have sounded off in my head, but it didn't, because I trusted him.

I continued to date Donovan and I completely forgot about the incident until I started to notice more signs of unfaithfulness. One night while Donovan was at my house for movie night he went upstairs in one of the guest bedrooms and I was left sitting on the couch watching the movie by myself, because he said that he had to take care of something. After about an hour passed, I tiptoed upstairs to see what was taking him so long to come back downstairs to watch the movie with me. He had the bedroom door closed and he was whispering on the phone at 12:30AM. So, I opened the door all the way and stood in the doorway to make sure he could see me standing there listening to him. I could hear a female voice in the background. Once Donovan noticed that I was standing there he jumped as if I startled him and quickly got off the phone. When he got off the phone I asked who he was talking to on the phone at 12:30 in the morning. He told me it was a friend from work. When I asked what they were talking about at 12:30 in the morning, Donovan said they were talking about the bible. I then said, "What scripture, or what specifically were you all talking about in the bible?" Donovan looked stunned that I continued to ask questions and he avoided answering my question by saying, "Why are you acting like you can't trust me and I can't talk on the phone?" I explained to Donovan that it looked suspicious, because he was whispering on the phone at 12:30AM to a "friend" that I've never met or heard of before. Donovan and I knew each other's friends. I understood that he had several female friends, which I didn't mind as long as I knew them. I had a mixture of male and female friends that Donovan knew. This particular incident sent up a red flag because I didn't know her and he was being evasive. Donovan could never tell me specifically what they were talking about in the bible, because I caught him off guard. He was never a good liar.

    I completely disregarded the whole incident for the next couple of months. Now, going back to about a week before the actual break up there was another situation. Donovan and I were supposed to be going out to a restaurant called "Bay Breeze" to celebrate the fact that I just finished getting my full teacher's certification. Unfortunately, Donovan canceled those plans with me because he got caught up helping a video production and he was going to be busy all day long. I was a little disappointed because I was going to be going out of town the next day to visit my brother in San Diego and would not get the chance to go out to dinner with Donovan until later. Donovan came over after working on the video production all day long to help me pack since he was the master of rolling up clothes to make more space in suitcases. As we were packing, Donovan began to tell me about his day working with the video production. He started by telling me that he had to play a part in this Christian video because the person who agreed to act in the video did not show up. I've never known Donovan to act so I asked him, "What did you have to do?" He replied, "I had to sit in this car and pretend like this girl was performing oral sex on me." In a state of disbelief I ask "What… are you serious?" What kind of Christian film is this?" Then he went on to say, "It's not like you're thinking- her head was only down on my lap." At this point, I'm completely shocked by what he was telling me. I begin to ask him questions like, "How were you pretending?" He would say things like, "You know like closing my eyes and acting like I was enjoying it." Then I asked him, "How do you know how you are supposed to respond to oral sex if you are a virgin and never had any sexual experiences?" Donovan replied, "I've seen movies and videos." At this point, I don't know what to do because a million things were going on in my head. After the argument calmed down, I told Donovan that we would discuss this situation more when I return from San Diego, because I needed to think.

During the entire week I was in San Diego I could not stop thinking about the disturbing things that Donovan had told me. I began to pray to God, because I needed guidance on this situation and I was too embarrassed to talk to my mom about it. I told God, "I need to know if Donovan is the person for me and I need you to show me clearly." That was my prayer for the seven days that I was in San Diego, because I was at a cross road and I didn't know what to do. God began to bring back to my remembrance all of the red flags that I had ignored that occurred within the past year such as the late night phone calls, text messages, dinner meetings, and Facebook message. I began to feel like I was content with the way that I had allowed for deception to enter into our relationship without dealing with the problems when they arose. Don't get me wrong, Donovan was a Christian man and I was content in thinking he was my husband, but he was also a man. All humans make mistakes and fall short of God's glory. If God had told me to forgive Donovan and yes he was my husband, then I would have followed what God had told me to do. Instead, God spoke to me through a series of events. Little did I know, God was getting ready to speak loud and clear.

On my plane ride home back from San Diego I sat on the plane in silence praying to God the whole way back. I told God "Today is the day; I have to know if Donovan is my husband. You have to show me clearly what to do." I had a friend pick me up from the airport and take me back to the house. I called Donovan to let him know that I made it back into town. Donovan said that he was on his way over so we could talk.

Upon his arrival to the house, he came upstairs to the bedroom while I was unpacking so we could talk more about everything that happened. I told him that I didn't understand the whole oral sex Christian video thing, but we had to discuss our future. Donovan was being defensive and saying that the video was nothing and that I was thinking about it the wrong way. I simply stated that we needed to talk about our relationship beyond the video. Donovan took a seat on the bed as we were talking and I was unpacking. I started to bring up all of those situations that God had brought back to my remembrance. I reminded him that at the beginning of our relationship we didn't have any secrets and we would be able to look at each other's phones without worrying about the content that we had sent out or received. Now things were different, and Donovan would hide his phone away from me. I asked him why things had changed. I asked him about the late night phone calls and text messages from these girls that I had never met. I told him that I was confused because we used to know each other's friends, but now there was so much secrecy. Donovan didn't have much of a reply to anything until I said. I told him if there's nothing to hide then let's exchange cell phones like we use to. Donovan refused! At that point I knew I couldn't trust him the way that I use to trust him. Donovan gave me a reason to doubt his faithfulness. By this time I was standing near my door to the room when I said, "I think we need to go on a break from each other and do some praying about this relationship." Donovan did not like my reply and became very angry. It was almost as if he turned into another person. I hardly ever heard Donovan raise his voice, but this time when he yelled I felt like I couldn't even recognize him.

    As he began to argue with me about breaking up; he was getting angrier and angrier by the second. He started to pace back and forth near my bed because I was standing in the doorway. I told him that it was best for us to take a break away from each other because I had lost trust in him. Finally, Donovan started moving towards the door and I was still standing there with my arms crossed at this point. Donovan shouts at me, "Move out of my way!" I looked him in his eyes and said, "No." Donovan then grabbed me and pushed me out of his way onto the closet door. He put his hands around my neck and began to squeeze tightly as he yelled, "I hate you!" I had never seen the amount of anger that I saw in his eyes before. I gathered my strength to push him off of me so I could breathe. Donovan went into the guest room to cool off, while I caught my breath. After catching my breath, I realized what had just occurred. I went into the guest room and with all of my strength, I punched him in the jaw and said, "Don't you ever put your hands on me like that again!" I then said, "Get out of my house now!"

Donovan went outside to his car and sat in his car. At this point, I knew that our relationship was over. I began to gather his stuff that was around my house and put it in a trash bag. I sat the trash bag on the porch and went to his car. Donovan then said, "Here, you can look at my phone now if that will make you happy." I replied, "No, but I put some of your belongings in a bag on the porch that you can grab before you leave." I didn't want to look at the phone anymore because I knew he was sitting outside in his car deleting text messages and call logs. Donovan then said, "I hope you didn't touch my stuff." Donovan stepped out of his car and started to walk towards the trash bag, while I was walking behind him. Donovan looked at the bag and turned around pushed me down the stairs off my porch and said, "I told you not to touch my stuff!"

I laid on the concrete not moving for a while and just kept looking at the grass. I could not believe what just transpired. First, he tried to choke me and now he pushed me down the five wooden porch stairs onto the concrete. Donovan frantically called his parents because he is afraid that I was seriously hurt. As I tried to muster enough energy to move off of the concrete, I heard Donovan telling his parents, "She accidently fell down the stairs." As I'm able to get up I started to shout, "No, you pushed me down the stairs; tell the truth! Tell the truth!" Donovan gave the phone to me as I began to talk to his Dad. His Dad asked me what happened. I started to tell Donovan's Dad how he pushed me down the stairs. His Dad asked what Donovan was doing now. I told him that Donovan was pacing back and forth in my living room. I could hear his mother saying, "I told that boy to leave the house already and come home!" I handed Donovan back his phone and he left.

  I took a picture of my neck, because you could see Donovan's hand prints around my neck. His handprint formed a bruise around my neck and eventually a scab. I called my mother to explain to her what happened and asked her what to do? She told me to calm down and to try to think clearly. I definitely didn't want to call the police and get the police involved in this matter, because Donovan and his family had been so good to me over the years. My mother advised me not to see Donovan again. I told my mother that my plan to stop dating him was what sparked the whole incident.

  I couldn't sleep at all that night. I just cried and cried. I was able to call several of my prayer partners in the middle of the night to pray with me. The next day I had to go to work, which was difficult because I was up all night long. I tried to cover my neck with make-up. I truly felt like one of those battered women that you see on TV or read about in the newspaper. I couldn't believe this was happening to me. There were no signs that Donovan would snap and turn violent in the three and a half years we dated. I was at a loss for words.

During the next week, I was in deep prayer with my prayer partners. We prayed for Donovan and what he was going through. It seemed like Donovan had turned into a different person at the time of the incident. God brought my prayer back to my remembrance, "I need to know if Donovan is the person for me and I need you to show me clearly." I even told God on the plane ride home that, "today was the day and I had to know today." It was almost like God was saying, "Do you have any questions now?" I've always said that I could never marry or be with a person that put their hands on me, so if I'm truly a woman of my word, then that would mean that I couldn't be with Donovan. God had clearly answered me on the same day that I came back from San Diego. My prayer to God now was, "Please lead and guide Donovan back to right standings with you and allow my heart to forgive him."

A week before Donovan's tragic accident he called me. I was surprised to hear from Donovan, because I thought I would never hear from him again. During the phone call, Donovan asked me to forgive him for his wrong doings. I told him that I had already forgiven him and I wanted him to forgive me as well. The only thing that I wanted Donovan to do was to be honest with his parents about the whole incident. Donovan made it seem as though I was at fault or to blame for the whole situation, when both of us played a part in it. We were both wrong in the way we handled the situation. When I noticed that Donovan was angry and pacing back and forth I should have stepped out of his way, but instead I antagonized him. Donovan should have never put his hands on me. We were both guilty of a lot of things, but we both knew that we still loved each other. After being in a relationship for three and a half years you develop a deep relationship with a person that is bound together by love. I believe that love can conquer everything- even life's most difficult situations.

  I remember the day before his accident, I was on my way home from church that day, and I remember seeing a car like Donovan's three times before I reached home. Tania called me up and I expressed to her how much I missed Donovan and how hard it was going about my life from day to day without him. I was so used to seeing Donovan every day and it was hard to not see him anymore. I guess in the back of my mind I felt like we would be able to get over this and at least become friends in spite of everything that occurred. While we were dating we were the best of friends. We shared a lot of experiences together. From going out of town to visit my family, taking classes at church together, and receiving the Holy Spirit with the evidence of speaking in tongue together. Our relationship was not superficial, but it was deep and one mistake couldn't destroy our love for each other.

After everything was said and done, I traveled to the funeral with his family several days later. This was the first time that I had ever lost anyone that I had a close relationship with. After families travel back to their respective families and your friends stop calling you to check on you to see how you are doing, because life for them goes back to normal; your pain is still there. The only person that I had to turn to was God. When you lose someone you love you can't just get over it after a couple of months. You go through a grieving process that takes several years. I thought I couldn't make it through but just when I was about to give up God stepped in and made me realize I was not alone.

God made me realize that Donovan was not gone forever, but he was a spirit. Just because you lose someone in the natural doesn't mean that you can't communicate with him or her anymore. When you lose someone in the natural, it means that your relationship changes. I understood that I carried Donovan within my heart. Every time that I think of Donovan and speak out loud to him I know that he can hear me. Donovan may not be able to respond to me in the natural, but I know that he hears me. Just as God hears us when we pray in the spirit I believe that you can speak to those that have passed on into the afterlife. We have to believe in our hearts that God hears us, because sometimes God doesn't speak to us audibly. Even if you've never heard the voice of God you still pray to Him believing that He hears all of your prayers for those that are in Christ Jesus. I believe God will allow for those that have passed on to hear us speak to them but He doesn't allow them to speak to us in the natural. I'm not saying that's it's impossible, but I'm only speaking from my experiences. I've spoken to Donovan in dreams, and he's spoken back to me, but again that's not in our natural being of everyday life. I would like to encourage anyone that has ever lost a loved one to speak to them-especially if you have any unresolved issues.

    Sitting back and reminiscing on my past I realize the ways in which God was speaking to me and answering my prayer. Through the entire year that I was seeking God's face about the future of our relationship God was showing me signs that Donovan was not the one for me. I didn't receive any of those signs, because I felt that Donovan was a great Christian man. I was content with Donovan and he was content with me. Although I loved Donovan and wanted him to be my husband God had different plans for me. God knew when Donovan's last day on this earth would be and I believe everything was orchestrated in God's timing. With his last month on this earth, Donovan was able to spend the majority of his last days with his family. His mother was able to tell him how much she loved him, embrace, and kiss him. God knew that losing Donovan would be a hard blow for me so we were destined to break up before the tragic event. Even though the break up didn't lessen the pain; it was easier to deal with the pain since Donovan had removed all of his belongings out of my house; so it didn't constantly remind me of the pain.

Going back to the week before the accident God had given me a dream of the large hand that I mentioned earlier in the book. I started to understand more of the meaning of the dream after reflecting on the events leading up to Donovan's accident. God was holding my hand as I grieved the loss of Donovan. Even though I felt as if my life was over; God had different plans for me. God would be guiding me through my journey while holding my hand through it all. I could not just give up on life, but I had to keep running towards the mark. Where exactly is that mark? I'm not sure, but I'm still discovering more about my purpose on this earth. I'm still committed to God taking me at my word. My prayer for you is that you learn to trust God no matter what you are going through in life.

FORGIVENESS

Forgiveness is deeper than saying I'm sorry.
Forgiveness is a three syllable word that goes deeper than the ocean.
Forgiveness is harder than running a 3K marathon.
Forgiveness is an action and not a phrase.
Forgiveness takes everything inside of you to not only say the word but to act on it.
Forgiveness can help you conquer any trial that comes your way.
Forgiveness and love are two of God's favorite nouns.
Forgiveness will confuse every attack from the enemy.
Forgiveness gives you unspeakable power.
Forgiveness frees you from anger and sin.
Forgive, forget, and live life to its fullest.

CHAPTER SEVEN

THE PROPHECY

It seemed like everyone had moved on with life while I was still struggling with my grief. I occasionally glanced at Donovan's Facebook page just to see his smile. I kept fearing that I would forget what he looked like, how he laughed, what he smelled like, and how his voice sounded. It was almost as if I was aware that I had dementia and each day I wonder what memories I would have forgotten. You know that the inevitable is bound to happen; you will slowly forget the little things; the things you don't want to forget. I soon had to come to the realization that life must still go on. Everyone was moving on with their lives and it wasn't that they had forgotten about

Donovan, but they had to learn to cope with the grief while moving on with their lives.

    I struggled at first moving on with my life. Everything that I did reminded me of Donovan. When I had to go back to work to start another school year I remembered how Donovan had always helped me set up my classroom, but this year I would be setting it up by myself. Some days I just simply cried because I would have a flashback to a memory of Donovan and me. For example, Going to the grocery store was hard, because I would think about all of the things Donovan loved to eat such as organic foods. It felt like my world was stuck in a place where I couldn't move on, because life had me stuck in a grieving state over his life. I felt stuck until my brother's wedding in San Diego, California.

    Weddings are the most beautiful sacred events for most people. However, for some people weddings can be depressing if they are lonely and don't want another reminder that they are alone. At the time, I was one of those people who struggled to be happy at the wedding because of the pain that I felt. Donovan and I spoke of marriage and he had planned to propose to me when the time was right.

    I tried to put on a smile for my brother and his soon to be wife, but a mother knows best. My mother was with me through it all. She was there for me the entire time when I lost Donovan, even when no other family members came to Atlanta for the funeral. My mother could tell that I was having a hard time being happy for my brother. I was still putting on a smile and laughing with my brothers and sisters. I just knew that my wedding day would be far in the future if at all. The day before my brother's wedding day my mother told me that God had spoken to her and told her, "It would not be long before I meet my husband and that when it happens it's going to move fast." I remembered those words just like it was yesterday. I can admit that when she said it I was a little skeptical, because I couldn't see anyone in my past being my husband. I was definitely nervous about meeting someone new and having to get to know someone all over again. I dated Donovan for three and half years, and I couldn't see myself dating someone else for another three and half years.

  The wedding was beautiful and everyone was having a great time at the reception. The food was delicious and everyone was partying. It was time for the garter and the bouquet toss. They called all the single ladies to the dance floor. I reluctantly went to the dance floor not anticipating catching the bouquet. All the rest of the girls were excited about trying to catch the bouquet, but I said to myself, "Let's get this over with." My brother's wife tossed the bouquet and it landed right on my chest. The bouquet slowly rolled down my body and fell on my feet. I was expecting some of the other ladies to try and snatch the bouquet from me, but they all seemed to back away from the bouquet. So, I slowly picked up the bouquet. The old superstition says that if you catch the bouquet at the wedding, then you would be the next person to get married.

After the wedding I went back to Atlanta, and re-evaluated the people I had in my life. I knew that the people that were trying to get back into my life were not my husband. It was almost as if they were currently in my life just to fill my lonely void. Unfortunately, I got attached to one person that was trying to pursue a relationship with me, but I soon ended it after God confirmed with me that he was not my husband.

Still, those words that my mother told me played back in my head. That winter we had a terrible ice storm in Atlanta. If you know anything about Atlanta, any sign of ice or snow shuts the entire city down until it thaws or evaporates away. This particular ice storm shut Atlanta down for an entire week. During that time, I spent a lot of time with God. I was praising, worshiping, reading my bible, and praying to God. I felt so close to God, because my life was still and I could just spend time with

Him. During my prayer time I prayed for my future husband. I was even thanking God in advance for my husband and praying for him. I was calling out all of the characteristics I wanted my husband to have. I told God that I would just trust Him through it all. I can still remember feeling the hand of God just like in my dream, and God revealing to me that He was going to be with me through it all.

On the Friday night after the ice storm was almost over I called up one of my friends. I expressed to her my frustrations of being alone. I was living in a nice three-bedroom-house by myself. I told her, I was tired of waiting for my husband and tired of being alone. I felt that Donovan was my husband and we dated for almost three and half years! I told her I couldn't see myself meeting someone and waiting for another three and half years. I told her how I'd been praying and thanking God in advance for my husband. At the end of the conversation she said, "You are still young and I've been waiting longer then you, so don't give up hope."

After getting off the phone with her, I made up in my mind that I was not going to give up. Sometimes I think when we start to become impatient, our blessings feel prolonged. Little did I know my blessing was right around the corner.

Literally, only two days passed before I met my husband.

TRUSTING GOD

Learning how to trust God is the hardest thing you have to learn to do.
As humans, we want to know the how, and the when will God answer our prayers.
Trusting God takes patience, which can mean months, or years.
Trusting God sometimes takes longsuffering, which means you might have to suffer for a long time.
Trusting God means walking by faith, and not by sight.
Trusting God might mean that you can't see with your natural eyes in ten feet in front of you, but if God says go then you must go.
I've learned to trust God through my pain and my fear.
I've learned that if you trust God, He will answer you and guide you through life's journey.
I've learned that if you trust God, He can do a quick work in your life.
I've learned that if you trust God, your life will be better than you could even imagine.
Thank you God for being faithful to me.
I call you faithful and trustworthy.

CHAPTER EIGHT

MEETING MR. RIGHT

On Saturday, my car broke down and I had to get it towed to a car shop. I wanted to go to church on Sunday so I had to find someone to give me a ride to church. I called up my friend Josh, since he lived close to me and asked him to give me a ride to church. Josh agreed but was late picking me up so I knew we would be in the far section of the church when we arrived. Josh had his niece and nephew with him that Sunday. I called one of my friends to save us a seat at church since I knew we were late.

Since it is a big church we had to park in the far away parking lot and catch the church bus to the front door of the church. Once we arrived at church, the Bishop was already preaching and the sanctuary was full. The ushers tried to stop us from coming into the sanctuary, but I explained to them that we had friends saving us seats. We walked upstairs in the back hallway to get to our seats. I was holding Josh's nephew, and he was holding his niece. We finally saw our friends, and we began to walk down the stairs to our seats. As I walked down the stairs, I began to trip in my three inch heels while holding Josh's nephew. All I could do was break our fall and grab onto a lady sitting in one of the seats. Thankfully, we didn't tumble all the way to the bottom of the stairs, but I managed to sprain my ankle in the process of getting to our seats. After we finally sat down, I took my shoe off because I could feel my foot swelling. I could not believe how awful my weekend or day seemed to be turning out. I tried so hard to make it to church, but it seemed like everything was trying to stop me from going to church.

     If you ever have a weekend like mine, then I advise you to keep pressing on through the chaos. Usually, when bad things continue to happen to you, then you have a blessing on the way. I didn't know that God was about to answer one of my prayers that I've prayed about for so many years. Little did I know, I was going to meet Mr. Right on that day. Only five months after my mother prophesied to me I finally met Mr. Right, and it was just like she told me it would happen. My mother prophesied these exact words to me, "It would not be long before I meet my husband and that when it happens it's going to move fast." Five months was definitely not long at all before meeting my husband.

Let's rewind back to the Sunday where I sprained my ankle at church. After sitting down and taking off my high heels I thought to myself, "Why did I even come to church today? First, my car broke down and I have to pay $700 to get it fixed, and now I just sprained my ankle coming late to church." I thought to myself, this day has to get better. There must be a blessing on the way with all of this stuff going on in my life right now.

At the end of service I waited for everyone to leave out of the sanctuary while talking to my friends that were sitting around me. Josh had arranged for one of his friends to give me a ride home, because he actually lived in my neighborhood with his mother. While I was talking to my friends I noticed this man standing by the drum set staring at me while we were talking. This man walked outside of the sanctuary after making eye contact with me.

Finally, my friends helped me limp down the stairs while carrying my bags and coat because my ankle prevented me from walking very well. I limped through the exit doors of the sanctuary into the hallway where I noticed the same man that was staring at me talking to the guy that was going to give me a ride home. I jumped into their conversation just to be friendly and to thank Josh's friend for offering to give me a ride home. They were talking about their plans for continuing their education and work.

Suddenly, the man that was staring at me reached out his hand to introduce himself to me and said, "Oh, by the way my name is Ryan Moore I don't believe we've formally met." I replied, "Hello, my name is Latoya McCants." Before I could get the next word out, he said, "I know who you are- I mean I've seen you around church (During that entire time we were still holding each other's hands and staring into each other's eyes)." I believe that was the moment I knew he was my husband.

My mother had always told me that when I met my husband, then I would just know. There was something about that moment when we locked eyes and held each other's hands that I knew he was the one. It was almost as if we were staring into each other's souls. I guess it's true what the old English proverb states, "The eyes are the windows into our souls." It's hard to explain, but if you've ever experienced meeting your spouse in a similar fashion then you understand what I'm talking about. I believe some people refer to it as, "Love at first sight," but it was more than the beauty on the outside. Our holy spirits had connected with each other and it was a divine appointment arranged by God. Josh's friend that was going to give me a ride home interrupted us by clearing his throat as if to say, "Hello, I'm still here." I didn't know at the time that Josh's friend had a crush on me and he didn't like what he was seeing.

    We stayed and talked for a while before Josh's friend Larry was ready to leave with his mom. His mom worked for the church so she sometimes worked a little late on Sundays. Larry's mom shouted at the young men standing around, "Don't you all see she needs help with her bags to the car? Someone grab her stuff!" Ryan grabbed my coat and bible as I limped out to the car. One of the security guys and Ryan helped carry me to the car since it was cold outside and I didn't have on any shoes.

    Later on that evening I got onto Facebook to check my messages and noticed that Ryan asked to be my friend on Facebook. I confirmed his friendship on Facebook that same night. Monday evening after work I got onto Facebook again and began looking at Ryan's Facebook page. I noticed a blog that he wrote on his page titled

"The key to a perfect relationship." I was intrigued by the message that he wrote on his page. He wrote this blog on May 4, 2010 and no one had made a comment on his page. Below is what Ryan Righteous wrote in his blog.

"I knew as a little boy that woman would always be my greatest challenge. And as I got older I learned that nothing happens in relationship unless God has allowed for it. My Pastor, Bishop Bronner has always put it in a way that he says you have to make love to Jesus first, get intimate and passionate with Him. That requires you to sit at His feet, and to worship Him in spirit and in truth in order to qualify for His blessings. Just like welfare, no one just receives it; they have to qualify for it. I'm one of the ones that believe I have to qualify for my wife. In that I believe that God has to flush me of my indiscretions i.e., a wondering eye, selfish desires, uncontrolled lust that must then be converted into love, also any unwillingness to compromise, or dishonest ways, just to name a few. I believe Christ is the head of the relationship and that our relationships are actually called His marriage, His family, and His children and so on. So then we must begin by honoring His presence by what Paul talked about in Corinthians, "Know ye not that your body is the Holy Temple, and you should not defile your temple or any of its members." (1Corinthians: 6:19) In the next chapter Paul goes on to say," It is good for a man not to touch a woman. Nevertheless because of sexual immorality let each man have his own wife, and each wife her own husband."(1Corinthians 7:1-2)

I believe our radio show and a couple of friends have figured it out. The key to a successful relationship is Christ! If faithfulness serves as your "lock" and Christ serves as your "key" then the two make up the mechanics for a seemingly perfect relationship. Now we should approach every relationship as though we are standing before Christ. Picture this... He is standing with a woman holding her hand and a man walks up to them all and asked for her hand. Before Jesus lets her go with him, would He not say to the man,

"Please take care of my one and only (her name here), she is all that I have. Do you promise to provide for her and take good care of her? Also promise me you won't dare harm my little girl, cause her any intentional pain, cheat on her, or demean her in any way. I want you to give her the attention she requires, the family she desires, and love bond that is never to be broken. Now here are Christ final words, this is what clinches His decision to give her away. He says to the man "As you have done so with Me for all these years". And the man replies "Yes my Lord, you know that I will. I promised you that long before I met her." If a woman were to take a man home to meet her mother and let's just say the mother was always in the room throughout your entire relationship; out of respect for her mother or in front of her, he wouldn't dare part his lips to lie to her, nor would he cheat on her, hit her, verbally abuse her, or refuse anything from her. Well that's the same way I view God. Out of respect to Him I would hope not to do any of those things to another person that He would not approve of me doing in front of Him or to Him. If I qualify with Him and I honor all these things in my relationship to Him, than when she comes along she is just added to us and now the relationship becomes as ONE when the three relationships are fused together.

You know what bugs me the most about relationships? I've done the math and polled this question. I would say that on a scale of 1-100 sex and intimacy in this day ranks at an all-time high of 70% of relationships make up. Funny because it seems that sex causes 70% of breakups as well. The most disturbing thing I've heard Christians say is that they plan to compare the person they end up with to the other people they've slept with. It's responses like that from Christians that cancel out God's intentions for the sex inside your marriage to be the most beautiful love-making you've ever had. It's at this point that your relationship is now spiritually disabled because you've just parted ways with the purity of the Holy Spirit and have given place to the flesh to re-live past sins, hurt, pain, and affliction. Perhaps you even have an insecurity or two that now your spouse has to deal with. Continue to work on your relationship with Christ so that when He qualifies the two of you, your relationship can go to the next level."

Love Always,
Ryan "Righteous"
The Field Trackstar

I commented on his page on January 24, 2011, the day after I met him at church. I simply stated, "Wow, that's powerful. I would love to hear more." I never thought that there were men still out there that had that type of mindset.

A few minutes later, I received a Facebook message from Mr. Ryan Righteous and within the email he proceeded to give me his resume. Ladies you know what I mean when men give you their resume about their life. Here is what he said to me:

"You're Welcome to Hear More Anytime!
Hi Toya thank you for reading my note(s). I was hoping to speak with again you sooner rather than later. Truth is I've spent the better part of my life learning how to build a relation in Christ. My notes just happen to be the fruit that has been produced during that time. If you didn't catch the conversation yesterday, I am a radio personality with a Christian Hip Hop radio show and a lot of what I feel is verbalized through public expression. I'll send you a friend request from that page. I and the other host take turns posting notes and we share our own personal blogs on that page and I would appreciate your support. On a more personal note, I would like to get to know you better. ☺ I'm looking forward to it actually."

At that moment I knew he was interested in getting to know me. To make the awkwardness less awkward for him I gave Ryan my phone number and told him that I would be up icing my ankle for a little while. Within ten minutes Ryan called me on the phone that night. One of the first questions he asked me was, "Why are you icing your ankle?" I said, "You don't remember me limping on Sunday after church? You helped me with my coat and bible." Ryan said, "I didn't even notice you were limping; I just thought you were really comfortable at church." I said to myself, "Wow, he didn't even notice I sprained my ankle." My mom said, "He was probably only focused on your face and not your feet." We talked on the phone for six hours straight. We talked about our families, jobs, goals, Christ, and previous relationships. I felt like we were able to get to know each other very quickly within one night. I even found out that the school that I worked at was a school that he previously attended when he was in middle school.

    Since he was recruiter for a college Ryan told me that he would be going to the high school down the street from my middle school and asked if he could stop over the next day. I told him when I had a free planning period and he said he would stop by my school. That night I probably only got three hours of sleep because we talked on the phone all night and I had to get up and go to work the next day.

Throughout the day, I had a huge smile on my face. There's nothing like knowing that the person that you prayed for all of your life has finally arrived. After walking my students to their connection classes I arrived back to my classroom. To my surprise, Ryan was standing inside of my classroom. Ryan was wearing a suit, with a suit coat, shiny black shoes, his face was glowing and he had his waves in perfect alignment. He was the definition of a "Debonair Man" very suave and refined. The first thing that he said was, "I brought an apple for my favorite teacher." Ryan pulled a green apple out of his pocket and gave it to me. I thought it was the sweetest thing that anyone had ever done for me.

We sat and talked for a while. It was a little awkward speaking face to face since we just spent six hours on the phone that night getting to know each other. Ryan decided to take a quiz that I just gave to my students. I helped him get a 100% on the test. I put a sticker on his quiz and sent him back to work.

Later on that night he called me up to let me know that he had some Epsom salt for my ankle. He came over my house with the Epsom salt and ran some bath water for me. He mixed the water and Epsom salt in the tub. He then put some rose petals in the tub. I sat on the lid of the toilet with my feet in the water. He rubbed my feet with the

Epsom salt and prayed over my feet for healing. I thought that it was the sexiest thing that anyone had ever done for me. Christian ladies know what I mean when we hear a Christian man pray. I said to myself, "God, he must be mine. This man is praying over my feet, rubbing my feet with Epsom salt with rose petals floating in the water!" Afterwards, we talked for a short while and he went home. We agreed that we both needed some sleep that night since we stayed up almost the entire night talking on the phone. We both were in school getting our Master's degree as well, so we had some schoolwork to complete that night.

After he left, I couldn't get any schoolwork done, because I had to tell my friends about him. I called my Mom first, because she has always given me Godly advice on every man that I've ever dated. I didn't want to waste any more time on anyone else that wasn't my husband; so if my Mom said he was okay, then I was going to continue to pursue him. I told my Mom everything that happened to me since meeting him on Sunday. She said remember what I told you, "It would not be long before I meet my husband and that when it happens it's going to move fast." I told my Mom that night that I thought he was the one. I explained to her about how our spirits connected with each other when we locked eyes on the first day that we met. At the end of the conversation she said that she would continue to pray about the developing relationship. Although, she didn't give me a definite yes or no answer she was already approving him, which is very rare for my Mom to approve of anyone I date. She told me that I needed to pray for myself, because God would speak to me just like He speaks to her.

I took my mother's advice and prayed to God. I asked God to immediately remove Ryan out of my life if he was not the person for me. Well, God never removed Ryan out of my life instead everything moved extremely fast.

We continued to either see each other every day or talk on the phone every day. On Sunday after church we went out to eat at Ihop. At Ihop he asked me to be his official girlfriend. He told me that I would be his first official girlfriend of 13 years. Of course, I said, "yes." I couldn't believe that I had a boyfriend. After I said yes, then I started second guessing myself. For example I asked myself, "Is it too soon for me to be dating someone seriously after Donovan? What will Donovan's family think about me dating someone else? What will other people think about me dating someone else?"

I told God, "Well I'm following your spirit Lord, and if you say Ryan is the one for me, then he's the one for me. I can't worry about what other people may say about me, because in the end it only matters what you think." It only took seven days for Ryan to ask me out to be his girlfriend, and we both knew we were each other's spouses. God was speaking to both of us. Other spiritual people in our lives were confirming everything about our relationship.

    I couldn't believe that God had that treasure hidden right under my nose. We both sat in the same section in church for years without even knowing each other. Ryan was such a catch; I couldn't believe that he was still single. There were many girls that tried to date Ryan, but he was picky and only wanted what God had for him. I admired that about him, because he didn't just settle with just anybody because he was lonely. Ryan was older than me so he definitely had to wait for a longer time than me.

    If I would have given up waiting on God that Friday night when I was on the phone talking to one of my friends about being lonely, then I would have missed out on God's blessing which was two days away. How many blessings do you think we pass up, because we don't have patience? You say you want your husband or wife, but you are with all those counterfeit men and women and giving them wifely and husbandly privileges. God can't step in and bless you with your man or woman of God if you are making your own decisions about who you want to be with, because God isn't moving fast enough for you. Sometimes I think God is saying to himself, "If my people would just trust me and see that I have their best interest at heart." However, we show God we don't trust Him when we spend time with men or women that we know are not our spouses. We only spend time with those people, because we feel as though it's the best that it's going to get. It's all about believing God's word, when He said to, "Seek ye first the kingdom of God, and his righteousness; and all these things shall be added unto you. (KJV Matthew 6:33)" God really means that He will add those things to your life when you seek His kingdom first. God will truly give you the desires of your heart. In Psalms 37:4. KJV it says, "Delight thyself also in the Lord; and he shall give thee the desires of thine heart." God will give you the desires of your heart when you delight yourself in Him. Some people say, "Well, I want Johnny even though I know he may not be the best, but I just want him." When you have truly submitted your life over to God, then you are delighting yourself in Him, and not doing what you want to do. You are constantly striving to please God in every aspect of your life. It's all about giving up the "I's" for "Christ." The "I's" are our selfish desires; the things that we see fit for our lives without consulting God. When you've taken on the mind of Christ, then your desires will become His desires. If your desires are like God's desires, then you won't want Johnny who smokes weed, or gets drunk. You would want that Godly man or woman of God that He has for you. Every person is not meant to have a spouse. Some people are meant to be single. You must be content with whatever God has for your life. It takes discipline of your flesh to truly serve God the way that you should serve Him.

  I had to learn how to discipline my flesh to make my spirit man stronger. I knew I had a weakness of not wanting to be alone. Because I didn't want to be alone, I would date counterfeit men just so I could go to the movies or out to dinner on a Friday or Saturday night. I knew in my heart of hearts that those men were not my husband. I had to grow and mature in my faith to learn how to be content with being alone on Friday and Saturday nights. I had to learn how to preoccupy my mind with reading my bible, learning how to play the keyboard, going out with my girlfriends, or exercising. I use to tell my friends that I was going to dress and look good for when I meet my husband. I concentrated on God and bettering myself while I waited for God to work in my life.

  Just remember that God will not send you your spouse until you are ready to meet him or her. Your spouse has to be spiritually ready as well. I had some growing up to do before I met my spouse. If I had met my husband five years ago, then I wouldn't have known how to treat him or how to act. I had to grow up spiritually and mentally to be prepared for him. Once I was prepared and my husband was prepared, then God orchestrated our meeting. I believe that if you haven't met your spouse yet, then God will clearly show you a sign when you meet him or her. It may not be a lock of the eyes, but God will show you and you will know when you meet him or her. My advice to you is to prepare yourself spiritually and preoccupy your mind with the things of God while you are waiting. Worship God with your life while you are waiting. Start thanking God in advance for your spouse and get intimate with God. Just don't give up on God, even if you have to wait years for God to answer your prayers. God will honor your faithfulness.

WHEN I FEEL LIKE GIVING UP

I feel like giving up when my family is stressing me out, and when I'm weary from worry.
Who's supposed to carry me through the storm when I'm in need?
When will I have my husband and my kids? God I feel like I'm getting too old.
I know your word says there's a season for everything, but I've been patient and true to you God, and I'm just wandering when is it my turn?
I'm constantly telling myself, "God will not put more than I can bare, and be strong; be of good courage and Lord shall direct my paths," but sometimes I feel like giving up.
I know I'm more than a conqueror, but God sometimes I get so tired.
And then, I remember…
I remember the footprints in the sand.
When I get tired from carrying all those burdens, you will carry me the rest of the way.
I know that you see and hear me crying out to you God.
When I cry; I'm taking my soul through a longing and cleansing of my soul.
Nobody is strong enough not to cry, my pride is not too much; I'm just letting you know that I'm still holding on.

And then, I remember…
I remember the childhood song, "1, 2, 3 the devil's after me, 4, 5, 6 he's always throwing sticks, 7, 8, 9 he misses every time, Hallelujah, Hallelujah, Hallelujah, Amen."
The closer I get to you God, the more the devil will attack me directly, or indirectly.
In the meantime, I remember…
I remember India Arie telling me to purify my soul and remember the little things.
The little things; I'm young, living for God, I'm in my right mind, I'm getting educated, I'm helping kids, I have a talented voice to sing praises to you, I'm healthy, I can walk, I can see, I'm beautiful, I have my parents, God you blessed me to see another year, and the list goes on forever more.
Now all I have left to do is to stand like Donnie McClurkin says.
In the meantime I will enjoy life, because your word says that you came to give us life and life more abundantly.
Every day I will laugh because I refuse to let the devil steal my joy away.
I'M A CONQUEROR; I WON'T GIVE UP!

CHAPTER NINE

SWEEPING ME OFF MY FEET

After the failed relationship with Donovan I knew exactly what prayer I needed to pray after I met Ryan. As you know, I didn't waste any time asking God to remove Ryan out of my life if he wasn't my husband. I asked God to clearly confirm that Ryan was my husband.

We continued to date each other and see or talk to each other every day. It didn't take long for us to get to know each other. We both were praying about our spouses and we both knew that we were each other's spouses. We met January 23rd, and Valentine's Day was right around the corner. I remember praying to God as a teenager and asking God for a romantic husband. Up until this point my dating life never consisted of a ton of romance. I sometimes received flowers, cards, or even fancy dinners, but nothing extravagant.

However, this Valentine's Day proved to be my best Valentine's Day I've ever had. Since Valentine's Day was during the school week we decided to have dinner on Sunday. Ryan took me to Ruth's Chris steakhouse, which was amazing. It was an intimate dinner setting with tasty foods. I already felt spoiled from the expensive dinner. Afterwards, we took a long walk in Centennial Park. We held hands and took pictures to remember that day. I thought I had a great Valentine's Day, but I didn't know Ryan still had plans for me on the actual day.

On Valentine's Day I woke up and got ready for work like a normal day. When I arrived at work and opened my classroom door I noticed something on my desk. Ryan previously asked my principal if he could come early to decorate my classroom with my Valentine's gifts. I saw a huge balloon with a teddy bear, cupcakes, a card, a figurine, a chocolate apple, and an edible arrangement. I'm usually a hard person to surprise, because I'm so nosy, but I was definitely surprised because I wasn't expecting anything else for Valentine's Day. I immediately called Ryan with shock and excitement in my voice. He was excited that I was so surprised. I told Ryan, "You've done so much for me already! I thought us going out for dinner at Ruth's Chris was all we were going to do to celebrate Valentine's Day." All day I was smiling, because no one had ever done anything like that before for me.

On my way home I called my mom to tell her about my day and she was excited for me. When I opened my door from the garage I walked into my kitchen to music. Ryan had his laptop up with a slide show playing for me. He had the Monica song, "Angel of Mine" on repeat. Ryan also had a Valentine's globe from the store "Things Remembered" on display for me. The globe was engraved "God's Gift, Angel of Mine, January 23, 2011."

At this point, I was totally blown away by how Ryan was spoiling me. I gave Ryan a spare key to my house since I lived alone without any close family members near. Apparently, after Ryan left from decorating my classroom in the morning he headed back to my house to set up the second surprise before going to work. I called Ryan again to express my gratitude and told him to come over. I made dinner for Ryan and we shared a nice intimate dinner together.

I called all my friends to tell them about my Valentine's Day and some were a little jealous, but happy for me. I could not believe how romantic Ryan was for me on Valentine's Day. I told God, "Wow, I did not know that you created a person like Ryan just for me!" God continued to confirm with me that Ryan was my husband.

Looking back on my list I created of wants and needs out of a spouse; Ryan had every characteristic that I prayed for years ago. The characteristics that I wanted were: sweet, spiritual leader, family man, hard worker, giving, kind, secure, safe, comfortable, mature, faithful, romantic, trustworthy, educated, go-getter personality, loves me unconditionally, sexy, gentleman, handsome, fun, and affectionate. I was very specific with my characteristics when I prayed to God. Some women pray about big muscles, light skinned, good hair, tall, perfect teeth, and broad shoulders. Some men pray about coke-a-cola bottle shaped body, long hair, light skinned, full lips, pretty smile, and pretty feet. If you are one of those people that's completely sold on the superficial, then you are not leaving God much room to work for you.

When you meet the person that God has for you; you will be completely satisfied without any hesitation. My Dad always told me as a child, "Some man is going to sweep you off of your feet." My Dad was right; Ryan swept me off of my feet like no one else ever did. For women; you should expect that your husband will sweep you off of your feet while you are dating. Ryan treated me as if I was the only person in the world that he loved and wanted to be with, and that's exactly how I felt. Your man of God should make you feel that way. Ryan was a gentleman and I loved how he treated his mother and sister. He even gave them special surprises on that Valentine's Day. I encourage young ladies to truly pay attention to how your potential spouse treats his mother and sisters. If he treats them with respect, then he will respect you.

  Men, when you begin to sweep that woman of your dreams off of her feet, then go all the way if God has spoken to you about her being your wife. Treat her as if she's the only woman you've ever had eyes for in your entire life. If she is your wife, then she will appreciate you and respect you. She will not belittle you, or think you are a push over.

  It's a beautiful relationship, because we are compatible with each other mentally, spiritually, emotionally and physically attracted to each other. Each day that God gives me to be alive; I pray for Ryan. I pray that God will continue to lead and guide him in every decision for our family. I pray that he will continue to seek God's face for our ministry. I pray that he becomes everything that God has destined him to be. I pray for his protection from all hurt, harm, and danger. I thank God for the treasure that He has given me. Ryan is like my Boaz.

The story of Ruth and Boaz reminds me of my life. Ruth was a widow, and her mother-in-law was Naomi. Naomi urged Ruth to go back to her home country where she could serve her gods. Ruth was determined to be loyal to Naomi and vowed to serve her God, which is the one and only true and living God. After realizing that Ruth was going to be loyal to Naomi they sat out for Bethlehem.

Once arriving to Bethlehem, Naomi remembered Boaz— a relative from her husband's side of the family. Ruth started to glean the fields behind the harvesters of Boaz's field. Boaz noticed Ruth in the fields and asked her not to glean any other field, but to stay and work with his servant girls. Boaz ordered the men to leave stalks behind for Ruth and not to harm her in any way. Ruth had found favor in Boaz's eyes.

One night, Naomi convinces Ruth to go to the threshing floor to uncover his feet and lie down. Boaz woke up in the middle of the night and noticed Ruth lying at his feet, which was a ceremonial request for marriage. Boaz was excited that Ruth was asking him to marry him because she could have chosen a younger man, or perhaps someone with more riches.

Boaz made plans to marry Ruth by first buying Naomi's property. In buying all of her property, then he was able to marry Ruth to maintain the name of the property, which was Naomi's deceased son. Boaz and Ruth got married and had a son. Boaz was Ruth's kinsman-redeemer as well as Naomi's, because he was a close relative of Naomi's that was willing to help keep her family possessions from being lost.

Ryan reminds me of Boaz, because he was like my kinsman-redeemer. He helped God in my restoration process. After losing Donovan, it was almost as if I became a widower like Ruth. I held on to my faith and trust in God, and found out that He is a faithful God. I was devastated when I lost Donovan, because I thought it was as good as it was going to get finding a Godly man. God did not let me down. God knows my past, my present, and my future. God had plans for me finding Ryan, my kinsman-redeemer. Ryan took my pain and nurtured me back to the place I wanted to be in my satisfaction of life. Ryan likes to say that I limped into his life, which symbolizes how Ruth laid at Boaz's feet to ask for marriage.

I'm grateful to God how He showed me that I was worth everything that Ryan had given me. Ryan treats me like a queen, and spoils me every chance he gets. You are worth waiting for your man or woman of God to sweep you off of your feet and appreciate you. Don't get discouraged if it doesn't happen as fast as you would like, or if the first or second "Christian" man or woman you date is not your spouse. There is always a plan and purpose for everything that occurs in your life. Remember some people come into your life only for a season, while others come for a lifetime. Don't get stuck in your winter and miss out on the beauty of enjoying every season in your life.

YOUR EYES

Your eyes pierced me from across the room.
You stood in the shadows of the corners of the room watching me from afar.
When we finally talked to each other outside the sanctuary and shook hands, I felt your spirit.
As we locked hands, our eyes met again, as if the world just paused for a split second.
It was a divine appointment set up by God.
What if I never tried to go to church because my car died?
What if I gave up and went home after tripping on the stairs on my way to my seat at church?
I would have never met your eyes, your face, or your spirit.
Your eyes are the windows to your soul.
I saw into your soul as you saw into mine.
Human words cannot encompass the connection that we made that day.
This is what it feels like to have a divine appointment set up by God.
Thank you God for the spiritual blessings that your give me.
Each day that I spend with you is a cherished gift from God
I Love You.
(To Ryan my valentine 2011)

CHAPTER TEN

GOD CAN DO A QUICK WORK

Ryan continued to sweep me off my feet by spoiling me with dates. He truly courted me just like I've always imaged a boyfriend would do. This was one of the happiest times of my life. We were enjoying our lives in the process of getting to know each other. I was blissfully happy and thanking God of the treasure that He had hidden for me. I knew Ryan was the one and he knew that I was the one for him. Once you know you've found your spouse, the next question is always, "When do we get married?"

To answer that question you must ask God. If you're a man and you don't have your finances together, then it's probably not the right time to ask her to marry you. However, if you have your finances together, you've confirmed it with God, and you've asked her parents for permission for her hand in marriage, then by all means go ahead and ask her to marry you. If we base our decision on what society says is the right time, then you might not be in God's will. Society might say that you need a year to get to know each other, a year to date, and then a year to be engaged, but if God says he or she is the one then there's no timetable. Ryan started taking me ring shopping in April to get my size, which was only three months into our relationship.

I knew Ryan would be planning a special way to propose to me so I was in no hurry for him to ask me for my hand in marriage. We continued to date each other for a while and I was working on finishing my Master's degree. I finished my Masters in May and was going to Boston, Massachusetts for the graduation on June 5th. None of my family members could travel to Boston for my graduation, so Ryan decided to go to Boston with me.

This was our first big trip out of town together. We went sightseeing and visited great places to eat like the Cheer's restaurant. Finally, it was graduation day and I was excited to be receiving my Master's degree. We celebrated with some of my fellow graduates and ate out at a nice restaurant. We then took a long walk to the "Walk Score of Saint Stephen Street" near the Fenway in Boston, which contained a beautiful fountain. The fountain gives an illusion of being a deep pond, but it's a flat fountain surrounded by beautiful cathedral-looking buildings.
     We sat in one of the benches at the fountain for a couple of hours just talking and enjoying each other. Ryan started talking about his finances and telling me that he was having a hard time saving money for a ring. I told him not to worry, but I would be patient in waiting for him to have enough money for a ring. Ryan then mentioned that we were supposed to go ring shopping and I was supposed to remind him that we needed to look at rings. I immediately said, "You didn't tell me that, because I would have remembered something like that!" Ryan said that it was ok and that we could go ring shopping when we got back to Atlanta. Ryan then told me that we had dinner reservations and we couldn't be late; so off we went for dinner. Ryan had dinner reservations at The Prudential Building at a

restaurant called "Top of the Hub," which was a luxury restaurant on the top floor of the huge skyscraper. The Prudential Building overlooked the ocean and the food at the "Top of the Hub" was exquisite. We noticed that the waiters were bringing graduates free desert with their meals; so of course Ryan told our waitress that I was a graduate too. Our waitress brought out a large bowl of ice-cream that had congratulations written in chocolate on the plate. My ice-cream was topped with strawberries and a pink candle.

    Before biting into my desert, Ryan suggested that we pray again to just thank God for the many blessing that He was continuously bestowing on us. Ryan grabbed my hand and started to pray and thank God for me reaching another milestone in my life. I started to notice that Ryan was repeating some of his sentences in his prayer and the prayer was getting longer and longer. When I opened my eyes I noticed a sparking ring sitting next to my ice-cream. Ryan then popped the question, "Will you do me the honor of being my wife?" I was speechless at first, but then mustered enough to say, "Yes!" I was so surprised and excited that he proposed to me. Everyone around us told me congratulations.

    Ryan then told me to call my Mom because she was waiting on my phone call. I called my Mom with excitement to tell her the good news.

She was screaming with excitement too. She couldn't wait for the phone call. Ryan asked my parents a couple of months ago if it would be okay to ask for my hand in marriage, and my parents said yes. My Mom even thought it was a good idea for him to propose to me while we were in Boston, since none of my family members could make it to my graduation. I then spoke to his Mom and his sister and they both congratulated me and welcomed me to the family. Ice-cream is my favorite thing to eat in the whole wide world, but I was too excited to even eat my ice-cream. We hugged and kissed each other.

  I was completely surprised, because we just talked about him not having his finances together and I told him that I would be patient and wait. I couldn't stop smiling and staring at my ring in disbelief of what had just occurred. Ryan proposed to me after four months of us meeting each other. I knew that nobody but God could make this process feel smooth and right after only knowing someone for four months. I had no doubt that Ryan was the one. I knew in my heart that he was the one for me.

  I called all of my closest friends to let them know that he proposed to me. It felt like a fairy tale. It was my very own fairy tale coming to life. I would have never thought in a million years that I would meet someone and five months later they propose to me. This was God's way of showing me that He doesn't move on man's timetable, but He makes things happen on His timetable. In the back of my mind as well as I'm sure other's minds, I was thinking, "Wow, I dated Donovan for almost four years and we didn't get this far in our relationship."

Again, I will say that everything that happens in your life happens on purpose, and with purpose. God knew that Donovan was not the spouse for me. If we had gotten married, and then he had a tragic accident early on in our marriage; I would have been even more devastated. There could have been a possibility of children growing up without their father. I don't have the answers, but all I know is that God knows our futures and when our last days are on earth.

God was able to show me that He could do a quick work. It doesn't necessarily take years for God to answer prayers, but everything happens on God's timing if you let God be God in your life. I had completely given my life and trust over to God. I trusted God for everything that was going on in my life. I was no longer trying to figure out the "Why did this happen to me?" I had to stop asking God, "Why and when" but I had to learn to just say, "Yes, God I will trust you." I learned to trust God no matter the season in my life; no matter how painful it might have been, I had to learn to just trust Him. If you could learn to trust God for whatever you are going through, then God can move in your life. He may not work as fast as He did in my situation, but you've got to trust Him and know that He will give you guidance for your life.

As humans we become impatient with God and we want God to tell us when we are going to meet our spouse. We want to know what day, and time. I think that sometimes God wants to surprise us. It's the surprises in life that makes life so interesting. Think about it- if we knew everything that was to come to pass, then life would be boring. Sometimes God just wants us to trust Him. However many of us try to be our own gods. We decide that God is not moving fast enough and we begin to just date anyone who looks shiny, but isn't the real jewel.

Some friends look at my life and say, "God, why can't you work like that in my life?" In order to get the place that I am in life; I had to go through some suffering and sacrifice. I had to learn to thank God in advance through my pain and tears. I had to learn to trust God even when everything in my life seemed so cloudy and dark. Every person has their own story to tell. You may meet your spouse and it may only take a month for him to propose to you; just don't put God in a box. Within a year, I met my spouse, dated him, got engaged, and got married.

When I would tell unbelievers about my testimony they would look at me crazy and say, "Wait, you just met him and you're getting married?" I would say, "Yes, when God says its time, then its time." Unbelievers couldn't comprehend how I could meet a man and know that he was the one in such little time. Some people date for ten years before they even get engaged, and then get married. Even being married after ten years of dating their marriage sometimes doesn't last long. I had so much ease when I married Ryan. I never got cold feet or nervous on my wedding day. We were both excited to consummate our marriage that night, since we were waiting. Our wedding was magical just like our relationship; my Dad walked me down the aisle and on the way down he whispered in my ear, "Are you sure you want to do this? You know you don't have to do this if you don't want to, because it's not too late." I told him, "Yes Daddy I want to marry him." The wedding party walked down the aisle to Monica's "Angel of Mine" which was the song playing on my laptop when I arrived home on Valentine's Day. I walked down to "Be Sure" by Karen Clark Sheard. The chapel was decorated in pink and brown colors with dim lighting. It was romantic and soothing. My youth minister from childhood conducted the ceremony. Afterwards, we took pictures and headed to the reception hall.

    During the reception we had an Impromptu lip sync to Marvin Gaye's "Heaven Must Have Sent You From Above." I was rehearsing the lines at the salon, because I had completely forgotten to memorize them. We even had some dance moves that were impromptu. The food was delicious, and I even had an ice-cream station at my reception. During our first dance we danced to "At Last" by Etta James, which had so much meaning to our lives. It seemed like we both had been waiting for our dream girl/boy to come and when we finally met each other it was a feeling of relief. We enjoyed our guests, took pictures, and then it was finally time to leave.

    Once arriving back to Atlanta; Ryan had to move back into his house, because he moved out to live with his Mom so I could live in his house so we could save money for the wedding. It worked out well, because I was able to decorate and paint the house to make it feel more like a home instead of a bachelor's pad.

    Looking back over everything, this was another joyous moment in my life. I was one of the happiest people on my wedding day. It's hard to describe the feeling that you have when you finally get something that you've waited for your whole life. Every day I continue to thank God for His many blessings and the favor that He has given me. I've learned that you must constantly remember the things that God has done for you to remind you how He answers prayers. Now, when I go through storms; my Holy Spirit is able to say, "Hey, you remember the time when you prayed for so many years and then God answered you." Each day that I spend with Ryan I'm constantly reminded of how good God has been to me. I'm reminded that I'm God's child, I'm His princess and God will take care of His children just like I would take care of my children. Now I understand the meaning of, "Count It All Joy." When you learn to count it all joy, then that means that you learn how to thank God for every situation that you experience, because God can turn it around for your good even if it looks bad. Thank you God for every experience in my life, because I'm enjoying the journey. Your journey may have some twists and turns, but stay the course. If you stay the course, God will give you the desires of your heart when you stay faithful to God.

TOGETHER

Words can fade away and become a distant memory
But the heart knows no end to its time
Distance can come between two people
But love finds its way back every time
You took a chance with an "unknown soldier"
Committed to doing battle in the army of the Lord
I can't promise I'll win every argument
But I can promise to lead your hand without fear or doubt
My love expression goes beyond any words
Beyond private and public displays of affection
It's even beyond this natural world
I think it's somewhere near His throne
Because the love I have for you I'm not yet worthy to own
It's our God who created our love
And the perfect definition is He
I can only hope that one day He entrusts your love to me
I love you with all my heart
Well with all the pieces you mended together
I know I'm the easiest man to love

But God equipped you to handle my weather
As long as we're submitted to Christ Then
we'll make it "No Matter What" Together!!!
By: Ryan Moore

CHAPTER ELEVEN

LEARNING TO TRUST GOD

I know that some people get tired of hearing, "You've got to just trust God," but I've learned just how true that statement is. Trusting God is more than just saying the words, "I trust you God." When you truly learn to trust God, then you show God with your actions. It's kind of like how faith without works is dead. Well, trust without any action is doubt, and God can't bless someone who doesn't believe that He will come through for them.

    First and foremost Ryan and I had to trust God's timing. With meeting Ryan so quickly and with him proposing to me after four months people could think that we were crazy. Sometimes when God tells you to do something it may sound crazy, but you have to trust Him anyway. Most people who thought it seemed crazy were worldly people and could not understand how God could work so quickly. We trusted God when we set our wedding date. For the people that were in tune with God; they were able to confirm that everything was occurring on God's timing. God will always send confirmation when He speaks to you. Confirmation may come through other people, situations, and dreams. Your spirit will even be at peace when you are in His will.

    After being married for five months, then God began to speak to us about the next transition in our lives, which was a new place to live. We were living in Ryan's two bedroom house after we got married, but we both knew that we would quickly outgrow that house. We began the house hunting adventure.

    It took us about a month to find the house that God wanted us to have here in Georgia. It was a beautiful house. It was three stories, five bedrooms, and three and in half bathrooms, sunroom, hardwood floors, and it had a creek in the backyard. We thought to ourselves, surely this is out of our price range. We prayed on it and said to the Lord, "Let your will be done. God, what you have for us is for us." We placed our bid on the house and God showed us favor in every way imaginable. There were others that bid on the house, but we out bid on the house by three hundred dollars. God had given our real estate agent and us the wisdom to know what to do in order to get the house. We were able to win the bid, but that wasn't the end of the journey. If you've ever brought a house, then you know the closing process can take up to a month or two before you actually get the keys to the house.

I had recently taken a step out of faith and decided to transfer from teaching at a middle school to a high school. After the school year ended I received an Interview with a high school only about two weeks after school ended. I was offered a position at the high school and I accepted the position. When you change jobs while you are buying a house it can be detrimental to you while you are trying to close on the house. Fortunately, the transition was within the time frame it needed to be in, in order for me to get a job and still declare that I was employed before the closing on the house. Everything was happening on God's timing. God had spoken to me about leaving the middle school and pursuing another location to work. I trusted and obeyed God and He came through right on time. I was able to have a new job and I was able to get a new house.

    I knew that it would be difficult in leaving from that school, because I did enjoy the relationships I built with my students. All of my students could see was that I was a dedicated teacher, but they didn't see what happened before and after school. I knew of the horror stories that other teachers told me when they tried to leave the school by transferring to another school. My principal would block them from leaving other schools by painting a horrible picture of the teacher, which in most cases was not the truth. As soon as she would find out that you were trying to leave, then it was time for harassment. She would come to their room weekly for observations to find things wrong with their teaching just so she could put negative things in their annual evaluation. She was very good at documenting, but she didn't always document fairly or accurately. The principal would continuously try to intimidate teachers by harassing them, which added more stress to their lives.

    Even though she tried to block me from leaving the school, God showed me favor.

Through continuous prayer daily, God made it possible that even with her horrible recommendation that she gave to the interviewing principal, I still got a new job at the high school. When my interviewing principal asked to speak with a different administrator; Ms. Elena the other administrator gave me all positive comments. In fact, everyone else that the interviewing principal talked to gave him all positive comments about me. God used that situation in my life to show me that He was still God and no one was bigger than him. All I had to do was trust Him and not let my emotions get the best of me.

      I was not the first person that she tried to use her power and influence to keep from getting a job. There were many complaints about her and grievances filed against her. Her defense was always that they were disgruntled employees. All of her evil doing was worthless in the end, because it didn't matter what she wrote or said about me. She would not get any credit for me being hired at my new job. God wanted me to know that He was giving me the job and not her. She thought that she was so powerful that she could plan and control everyone's life. She believed that no one could be promoted unless she said you could be promoted. There's no demon in hell more powerful than God. I was glad that I could continue to learn to trust God in spite of all the odds against me. I want to encourage anyone reading this to learn to trust God even when it seems hard. Trust him when you're ready for your flesh to act out and fight against someone. In the end; God always win. It may be difficult to see how He will work it out, but you have to just trust God to see you through your trials.

GOD CONQUERS EVIL

God always conquers evil.
Trust God with all your might and with all your soul and you will see that God conquers evil.
Beware of those that call themselves followers of Christ, when they are just fans of Christ.
Beware of those that quote scriptures and know the entire Christian lingo.
Beware of those that misuse their power of influence.
Beware of those that claim that Christ has spoken to them, but are false prophets.
God has given us assurance that He will be our defender against the evildoers.
God will use your enemies as your footstools.
God will be victorious in your life.
Trust God to speak to you to give you direction in your life.
God will order your footsteps no matter what man may think or say.
If God says to move, then move.
Men may not understand the calling on your life, but trust in God.
God holds the whole world in His hand.
God is the ruler of the universe.
God controls everything about our lives.
Trust I say, trust in the Lord.

CHAPTER TWELVE

GOD SPEAKS

Looking back over my life I have discovered that God speaks all of the time even when we don't think He's speaking or when we don't listen. If we would just stop to listen and watch how God is speaking to us, then we would find out that God was speaking to us the whole time. Some people believe that God doesn't speak audibly, or they don't understand the other ways that God speaks to us as believers. I've experienced many ways that God speaks to His people. He speaks through dreams, situations, relationships, people, and audibly. God will speak to you in a unique way; you just have to be prayerful in understanding the ways in which God speaks to you. If you look at Moses in the bible God spoke to Moses through a burning bush. God spoke to Joseph through dreams and gave him the gift of interpretation. God even spoke audibly. I serve the same God from the bible, which means He can do the same things that are recorded in the bible. God is still in the miracle working business. Through God's power as Disciples of Christ, God has given us the authority that He gave to his twelve disciples. As Disciples we can raise the dead, heal the sick, and cast out evil spirits. We are more than conquerors. Just as Christ was persecuted you better believe that as a follower of Christ you will also be persecuted.

   In this life you will have to bare a cross and each person's cross is different than the next. Your cross might be dealing with a sick loved one, financial struggles, or infertility. Whatever your cross is you must bare it every day. God didn't promise us that we wouldn't have struggles or disappointments in life, but He does promise us that He will never leave us or forsake us. The bible teaches us to take up our cross daily and die to our flesh. We must give up our selfish desires for Christ.

   At the time of Donovan's death I didn't understand why it happened to Donovan nor did I understand why I was going through this difficult situation as a young person in life. I felt like God was punishing me for something I did. I had to remember that God is a just God and everyone has an appointed time with death. Death is absolute and everyone must deal with grief. We will all face death someday. You might be a young twenty year old, a parent in your forties, or you may even be in your eighties. Whatever the age that God has for you is an appointed time just for you. We cannot control when we die or how we die. We must all be ready at all times. It's almost like being ready for His second coming. The bible teaches us that it will happen just like a blink of the eye. I think that's how death is, because one minute you are here and next you can be gone. You must get rid of all unforgiveness in your heart, and always have a spirit of repentance. You must be in constant prayer with God, because some of us will not be fortunate enough to always be in our right minds when God takes us away. Even when someone is sick in the hospital, we must understand how to pray for God's will-- rather that's for them to be healed or if it's their time to go. We can't change God's mind when it comes to death. My advice is to live with a purpose each and every day. Don't let a day go by in which you are harboring ill feelings about someone. Just learn to let it go and forgive them for your sake.

  In the dream God gave me before Donavon's passing I was on top of a hill and then running down the hill while this large hand was holding my hand. When I woke up from the dream I could still feel a hand holding my hand.

He knew that it was going to be difficult for me to deal with and I was going to have a lot of questions. God was preparing me in advance to let me know that He was going to have my hand the entire time. God was telling me that my race was not finished yet and I had to keep running for Him. God never left me, which helped me gain strength to continue this race.

Many people blame God for deaths of loved ones and because they blame God they turn away from God. I could not be that type of person that could just turn away from God, but I could see how it's possible for some people. For example, I think of people that have had loved ones on their death beds and they prayed to God for their healing, but God doesn't heal but instead He lets them pass. I think of people that lose loved ones from murder. I can just hear them yelling out to God, "Why God, why did you let this happen to them!" We must remember that God didn't bring evil into this world, but evil goes all the way back to Adam and Eve. When Eve and Adam ate the forbidden fruit; they introduced sin into the world. God had to send his one and only son into earth to die for our sins so that we could have the chance to have everlasting life. God never promised us that He would keep us away from hurricanes, tornados, tsunamis, murderers, or thieves. It rains on the just as well as the unjust. That's just the way the world that we live in works. This is why God is preparing a place for us in heaven for those that can fight the good fight of faith, stand up for God's morals, bring others into the salvation of Christ, and create more Disciples by letting our lives be witnesses to others.

It's hard to cope with the death of a loved one, whether the person who dies is young or old. Just remember that our spirits never die, instead they are transformed. Our earthly bodies may be destroyed by water, fire, decomposition, natural disasters, car wrecks, but our spirits will live on forever. The way in which you live your life is directly proportional to whether your spirit will end up in heaven or in hell. This life on earth is only temporary. Where do you want to spend eternity?

Through much prayer, I was able to get through the loss of losing Donovan. I can say that when you lose someone close to you; you go through grieving stages. You don't ever really get over losing someone, but time does heal all wounds. You may cry every day for the first couple of months when you think of that person, but then it may become once a week. Once you've accepted the fact that the person has transformed into another part of life; then you realize that your relationship does change with that person. Donovan visited me in several dreams after he passed away. In some dreams we would talk about my feelings, and other times we would talk about current things that were happening in my life. I remember in one of my dreams he was telling me that it was okay for me to go ahead and move on with my life because I had to keep on living. My purpose on this earth was not finished yet, and I couldn't get stuck in this spot in my life. When he told me that I did feel like I was stuck at that point in my life, because of all the connections I had made with his family and friends. I felt like I couldn't fully move on with my life, because I was still so connected with his family. It was after that dream that Donovan did not visit me in my dreams for a very long time until after I was married. I guess God knew that it was unhealthy for me to stay so attached to Donovan through my dreams, because I wouldn't have been able to move on with my life.

  During this time in my life I got very in tune with God. My prayer life had strengthened and I was content with being alone. Distractions started to come into my life with men who wanted to be in my life, but God quickly told me that they were not the one for me. I had to get rid of all the distractions before I met Ryan, my husband.

  God spoke to me when I met Ryan. I knew immediately that he was my husband. I had to learn that when God says its time, then its time. It doesn't matter what people say or think, but when God says its time, then go for it. When I met Ryan I was still grieving over Donovan, but I was in a different stage of grief. I had stopped crying every day and I had accepted the fact that our relationship had changed. Fortunately, Ryan is a man of God and could understand my pain. Ryan showed patience and understanding with me. He was not jealous and was okay with me talking about my feelings. I couldn't get over the fact that God continued to be good to me through all of our trials. God had given me the man of my dreams and I felt undeserving of him and his never ending Grace.

  I soon learned how God spoke and how God restores. Everything that I thought I had lost with Donovan, God restored with Ryan more than hundredfold. I'm constantly smiling with Ryan. We are growing spiritually together as he leads this household. God has done a quick work in our lives. After we met, we dated and got engaged about four in half months of meeting and we married only eleven months after meeting each other. We both were in tune with God and were completely comfortable with God moving so quickly in our lives. God blessed us to purchase a new house only after eight months of us being married. Now we are expecting our first child

Ryla only a year and five months after being married. God is truly awesome, because after dating Donovan for almost four years I knew for sure that it would take a long time before I would meet my husband.

If you keep living for God, then God will show you so many surprises in life. I've never been happier in my life, then I am right now. The older I get, the more wisdom I gain, the sweeter my life becomes because I'm still serving God. I can't imagine a life without God being my number one in my life. God has supplied all of my needs and He's continuously holding my hand as I run this race. I know that my race is not finished and I don't know when it will be finished, but I do know that I'm going to keep on serving God until my appointed time with death. God has been so good to me. God is merciful, loving, gives grace, my comforter, my friend, my heavenly father, He is everything to me.

This book started off as a journal that I was writing while I was grieving over the loss of Donovan. It evolved into a book as God was bringing revelation into my life. My prayer for you, the reader, is that you will find your unique way that God speaks to you. If you have ever suffered from a loss, then I want to encourage you to remember that there is a God of restoration. "The One Who Restores" all things as if they were new. He is the ultimate source of new beginnings. He is the God of love and He wants us to love and forgive others just as Christ did for us. Use my life as an example of how to forgive others when we have been wronged and to learn to love unconditionally, because love conquers all. Enjoy your journey, live your life, and be all that God has called you to be; in Jesus holy name, Amen.

GOD'S HAND

Trembling and shaking I will go into the valley of the shadow of death.
Trembling and shaking I will do the impossible.
Trembling and shaking I will be prepared for disappointment and grief.
Trembling and shaking I take one foot and put it in front of the other.
Trembling and shaking I will sing, write, preach, and praise your holy name in front of all men.
Trembling and shaking I will share my story.
Trembling and shaking I will make Disciples of men.
Trembling and shaking I dare to dream.
Trembling and shaking I dare to achieve what you have set forth for me.
Trembling and shaking I dare to find purpose and destiny.
Trembling and shaking I dare to succeed.
My trembling and shaking hands will be put to rest as I run this race as God is holding my hand.
With trembling and shaking I know I can do all things through Christ that strengthens me sayeth the Lord.

God's hand can calm a storm, wipe tears, catch you when you fall and pick you up again.
God's hand will forever be with you if you just learn to hold on to His hand.

www.ingramcontent.com/pod-product-compliance
Lightning Source LLC
LaVergne TN
LVHW011422080426
835512LV00005B/203